The Lace Knitting Palette

President and Chief Executive Officer: Rick Barton

Vice President and Chief Operations Officer: Tom Siebenmorgen

Vice President of Sales: Mike Behar

Director of Finance and Administration: Laticia Mull Dittrich

National Sales Director: Martha Adams

Creative Services: Chaska Lucas

Information Technology Director: Hermine Linz

Controller: Francis Caple

Vice President, Operations: Jim Dittrich

Retail Customer Service Manager: Stan Raynor

Print Production Manager: Fred F. Pruss

Vice President and Editor-in-Chief: Susan White Sullivan

Director of Designer Relations: Cheryl Johnson

Special Projects Director: Susan Frantz Wiles

Art Publications Director: Rhonda Shelby

Senior Prepress Director: Mark Hawkins

Produced for Leisure Arts, Inc. by Penn Publishing Ltd.

www.penn.co.il

Editor-in-Chief: Rachel Penn

Design and layout: Ariane Rybski

Photography: Roee Fainburg, Catherine Thomson pages 9-10, 61

Styling: Luise Bracha

Make up: Sigal Asraf

Hairstyling: Guy Samuel

Special thanks to www.shiluvimbateva.co.il

PRINTED IN CHINA

ISBN-13: 978-1-60900-317-3

Library of Congress Control Number: 2011931143

Cover photography by Roee Fainburg

The Lace Knitting Palette

by

CATHERINE THOMSON

A LEISURE ARTS PUBLICATION

Contents

Introduction

For some, your journey into lace knitting is about to begin. For those already familiar with lace knitting, be prepared, as you pick up your needles and new yarns, to enter a world of new possibilities. Today's yarns provide endless opportunities, and I have combined them with stitches from Shetland lace knitting and motifs and techniques of my own, to produce lace which is eye-catching and thought-provoking.

In today's busy world, our knitting time can be limited, but an innovative, streamlined approach to pattern design has been developed to produce bold and beautiful lace with the minimum number of stitches. Many of the pieces are designed for knitting-on-the-go.

My own journey in lace knitting has been full of fun and enjoyment, and continues to provide me with challenges as new yarns are produced with new characteristics. I was once asked to submit a piece under the theme, "We are at our most creative when we are having fun. "After some thought, I contributed a fine lace garter, knitted in fine waxed dental floss on the finest needles, and called it "Candy Floss". It stays in my work space as a constant reminder that lace knitting should be fun.

Let your own journey begin.

Catherine Thomson

About the Author

Award-winning designer Catherine M. Thomson learned to knit at age 6 in Scotland. After many years of knitting as an adult, she turned to designing hand-knitted lace. Recognized for the artistic quality of her designs, Catherine relies on intuition in the design process and the techniques she has developed as new concepts evolved before her eyes. Today, she's still on a pathway of discovery.

Catherine's work has been displayed in exhibitions in Canada and other parts of the world. Her works won awards in two sections in the 1999 American Knitting Guild lace section, Winner of the 2000 American Knitting Guild Millennium Design Contest, Lace Section and have been displayed in several exhibitions such as "Threads of Life - Culture of Cloth", B.C. Fabric Artists' Guild 30th Anniversary juried exhibition, Vancouver, Canada, January 2001, New South Wales at the Australian Cotton Fiber Expo 2001, "Taking Cotton into the New Millennium". In 2002 Catherine's lace design was awarded a Very Highly Commended at the Royal Highland Show in Scotland.

Abbreviations and Symbols

ABBREVIATION	SYMBOL	MEANING
bo	∩	bind off
bo	Ⱶ	stitch remaining after bind offs complete
co	c	cast on
increase 1 st	1	increase one stitch
k	▪	knit one stitch
kb		knit into back of loop
k1 into next st	♦	knit one stitch into the next stitch
k2tog	/	knit two stitches together
k2togb	%	knit two stitches together through the back loops
k3tog	↑	knit three stitches together
k4tog	4	knit four stitches together
p	—	purl one stitch
p back	¬	purl back
p2tog	Δ	purl two stitches together
p2togb	▲	purl two stitches together through the back loops
p3tog	Ⅲ	purl three stitches together
RS		right side
skp	\	slip 1, knit 1, pass the slipped stitch over
sl1 k2tog psso	Ⅱ	slip 1, knit 2 together, pass the slipped stitch over
slk	□	slip one stitch knitwise
sskp	Ч	slip, slip, knit, pass the slipped stitches over
WS		wrong side
yo	o	yarn over needle
yrn	◊	yarn round needle in purl stitching
	◄	knit row from right to left
	►	knit row from left to right
	▨	location of short rows where you turn before reaching the end of the row
	■	no stitch
( )		repeat stitches within ( ) the indicated number of additional times
*		repeat stitches within * * as indicated

Needle Size Chart

US	mm	US	mm
0	2.0	8	5.0
1	2.25	9	5.5
2	2.75	10	6.0
3	3.25	10½	6.5
4	3.5	11	8.0
5	3.75	13	9.0
6	4.0	15	10.0
7	4.5		

Techniques

Bind Off

Where a piece requires either a firmer or looser bind off than usual, this is indicated in the pattern. Sometimes a slightly larger needle is used for the bind off.

Cast On

Where a piece requires either a firmer or looser cast on than usual, this is indicated in the pattern.

Dressing

Dressing is the part where you see your lace knitting transform from a lumpy looking object to a beautiful piece of work. Dressing requires a light wash by hand, very gently squeezing your knitting. This removes any dirt. Finish by rinsing. At this point your lace is very pliable. Gently squeeze out excess water, and transfer the article to a towel and allow the towel to absorb the remainder of the water. The time in the towel varies depending on the weight of yarn and the size of the piece . Your knitted piece should feel slightly damp and free of any dripping excess water. You are now ready to pin out the lace. A thick piece of styrofoam and a freshly laundered bed sheet are ideal. Gently place your lace on to the sheet; your lace will have a natural shape. Slowly work the lace to the outer edges where the points are. By this time you will start to see the results of your weeks of knitting. Place a pin in each point working from side to side, the pins simply support the structure.

When you have finished, leave to dry naturally indoors. After about one hour check to see if it is completely dried, and if so take out the pins and remove from the sheet.

The complete dressing procedure can take many hours depending on the size of the piece. It has to be a continuous process, so set aside a day just for the procedure. As you start to unpin your lace you will be amazed at the transformation that happened during the washing and dressing process.

Loop and Ladder Lace Seam

This approach is especially important when working with very fine yarns where a hand-sewn seam detracts from the fineness of the appearance. The approach uses pieces with a yo k2tog on the RS rows and a k2 on the return rows, producing a loop. You are going to weave the loops from side to side.

An example is provided with one piece in blue and the other in yellow.

1. Place the two sets of loops side by side, RS of work facing, with the blue closest to you and pull one of the ends through both the yellow and blue right end loops and tie a knot.

Step 1

2. Insert crochet hook down through right-most blue loop.
3. Continue inserting hook through right-most yellow loop with downward motion and pull it through the blue loop.

Steps 2, 3

4. Go back to the blue side and insert crochet hook underneath the blue loop to pull the blue loop through the yellow loop.

Step 4

5. Go back to the yellow side and insert crochet hook down through the next yellow loop and pull the yellow loop through the blue.

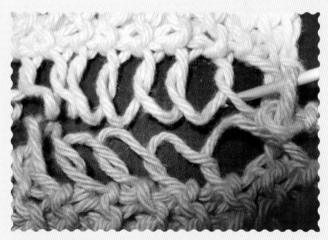

Step 5

6. Go back to the blue side and insert crochet hook from underneath to pull the blue loop through the yellow loop.

7. Continue in this way going from side, coming from underneath the blue loops to pull them through the yellow loops, and coming from above the yellow loops to pull them through the blue loops until there is only one loop left on the crochet hook. Bring the end piece of yarn through the loop and secure with knot and weave in ends on the opposite pieces.

Steps 6, 7

Finished Seam

Pattern Format

In the patterns, I have kept stitches associated with particular elements separate rather than running all the numbers together.

For example, in a row of the where there is a
"k2tog yo yo k2tog"
the row after would have "k1, k1 p1 into yos, k1" .
Running the numbers together would give "k2 p1 k1".

Stitch Line (Safety Net)

A stitch line is a piece of fine waxed dental floss or other yarn which is run through a knit or purl row at different locations using a weaving needle. It is like a safety net for any dropped stitches which cannot run beyond the line, allowing you to undo your work safely.

Tension Guidelines

Use the practice pieces and edgings to evaluate your lace knitting tension. For larger items where finished size is important, if your final practice pieces were larger than the dimensions given, go to a smaller needle size. If smaller, go to a larger needle size. The practice pieces will also allow you to evaluate other yarns you may be considering.

Useful Hints

• Needles are very much a personal choice. I use bamboo as well as needles specifically designed for lace knitting.

• For care of the finished piece, see the instructions on the yarn label - read the label before purchasing to see if hand washing is required.

• At the beginning of my knitting, I tie a knot in the yarn. When I come to weave in the end, I cut off the knot and have a firm piece to thread through the needle.

• For edgings and small items use short needles.

• Light colored yarn is easier for a beginning lace knitter.

• Lace can be made with needles from a size 2 mm (US 0) to a size 12 mm (US 17). Single ply and 2 ply yarn on very fine needles takes a long time to knit. Start big then go small.

• Lace requires a quiet area. It is like reading a good book - you are fully absorbed.

• Use lace to enhance other items.

• Look for lead stitches. The lead stitch is usually the middle stitch in the pattern; e.g. on a 7 stitch pattern, stitch no 4 will remain constant from the beginning to end. This is your guiding stitch.

• Looking at the construction of your pattern as you work the row will help you to see where you are going.

• Some patterns take a jog or Zig-Zag. These are a little trickier, but after knitting some beginning patterns give these others a try as they are well worth the effort.

• For beginning lace knitting, pick a pattern where every alternate row is garter stitch or purl stitch.

• Always join yarn at the beginning of the row.

• Looking back and forward to your pattern can be a distraction and can cause stitches to drop off your needles. If working on a 8 row repeat, try and memorize row 1 and 7 then 3 and 5 and in no time you will be able to work your pattern easily.

• If possible always complete your row. This allows for more even tension and less chance of dropping yarn-ons or stitches.

• Record the row you finished on and pop stitch stoppers on to the end of your needles.

• Yarn-ons are what makes the holes in lace knitting and makes the pattern beautiful.

• Charted patterns let you see what your lace should look like.

• Write patterns out in large letters so you can read it from a distance. Place on a small easel at eye level.

• Transfer patterns on to recipes cards and put them in a small plastic sealable sandwich bag. This way you can take your pattern with you and can read from both sides, and you can keep the original pattern or magazine in good shape.

• Bind off stitches should be worked with a needle one to two sizes larger to keep the lace loose.

• Good tension makes lace work easier. Keep your stitches on the feeder needle close to the tip of the needle. Keep a good grip on your yarn - this way your tension will be even. Keep your shoulders and neck and arms warm as you knit, especially in the colder months, and remember to shake out your fingers and move your neck during and after knitting.

• If you need to unpick your lace, use a needle two sizes smaller than the ones you are knitting with.

TRIMS

Circle Trim 1

MATERIALS
• 1 ball Caron Spa Acrylic and bamboo yarn, Rose Bisque.
85g ball (230m/251yds)

NEEDLES
• US 6 (4 mm), needle to weave in ends

SIZE
• To desired length

Instructions

Pattern 3 sts 4 rows

Co 3sts
Knit two rows

PATTERN ROWS
R1 k1 yo yo k2
R2 slk k2 p1 k1
R3 k5
R4 bo 2sts, k2

R4 ▶	∩	∩	Ⱶ	▪	▪	
	▪	▪	▪	▪	▪	◀ R3
R2 ▶	☐	▪	▪	—	▪	
	▪	▪	O	O	▪	◀ R1
	5	4	3	2	1	

Repeat to required length
Bo all sts

Circle Trim 2

MATERIALS
• 1 ball of of fine metallic yarn

NEEDLES
• US 2 (2.75 mm), needle to weave in ends

SIZE
• To desired length

Instructions

Pattern 3 sts 4 rows

Co 3 sts
Knit one row

PATTERN ROWS
R1 k1 yo yo yo k2tog
R2 k1, k1 p1 k1 into yos, k1
R3 k3 k2tog
R4 k2tog k2

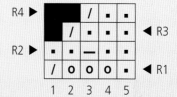

Repeat to required length
Bo all sts

Loop Trim

MATERIALS
• 1 ball Anchor Liana Metallic Cotton, Beige-gold. 50g ball

NEEDLES
• US 7 (4.5 mm), needle to weave in ends

SIZE
• To desired length

Instructions

Pattern 3 sts 4 rows

Co 3sts loosely
Knit 1 row

PATTERN ROWS
R1 k1 yo yo k1 yo yo k1
R2 k2 p1 k2 p1 k1
R3 k7
R4 bo 4 sts, k2

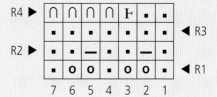

Repeat to required length
Bo all sts

Pointed Trim

MATERIALS
• 1 ball Patons Grace Yarn, Natural. 50g ball (125m/136yds)

NEEDLES
• US 6 (4 mm), needle to weave in ends

SIZE
• To desired length

Instructions

Pattern 3 sts 6 rows

Co 3 sts

PATTERN ROWS
R1 k3
R2 k2 yo k1
R3 k2 yo k2
R4 k2 yo k3
R5 k4 yo k2
R6 bo 4 sts, k2

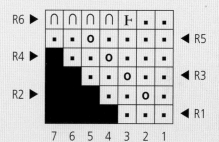

Repeat to required length
Bo all sts

Ric Rac Trim

MATERIALS
• 1 ball Caron Spa Acrylic and bamboo yarn, Berry Frappe. 85g ball (230m/251yds)

NEEDLES
• US 8 (5 mm), needle to weave in ends

SIZE
• To desired length

Instructions

Pattern 3 sts over 6 rows

Co 3 st loosely

Knit 1 row

PATTERN ROWS
R1 k1 yo yo yo k2tog
R2 k2 p1 k2
R3 bo 2st, k to end
R4 k1 yo yo yo k2tog
R5 k2 p1 k2
R6 bo 2sts, k to end

Repeat to required length

Bo all sts

	5	4	3	2	1	
R6 ▶	∩	∩	Ⱶ	▪	▪	
	▪	▪	—	▪	▪	◀ R5
R4 ▶	▪	o	o	o	/	
	▪	▪	Ⱶ	∩	∩	◀ R3
R2 ▶	▪	▪	—	▪	▪	
	/	o	o	o	▪	◀ R1

Edgings

1

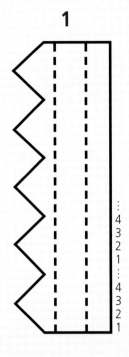

2
3

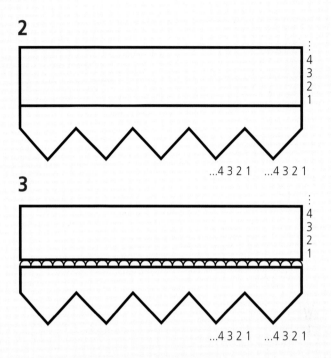

The examples I have included illustrate three approaches to construction of edgings:

1. Medallion and Ladder Edging (page 18): worked side to side

2. Scallop and Honeycomb Edging (page 20): the scallops are a trim worked from side to side and the shaping is contained inside the pattern stitches giving a smooth scalloped edge. The honeycomb section is then worked from bottom to top, with stitches being picked up from the straight edge of the scallop trim.

3. Pointed Edge, Eyelid and Holes Edging (page 22): the pointed edge trim is worked from side to side. On odd-numbered rows the yo k2tog provide a loop. These loops become stitches when picked up to continue the next section from bottom to top.

Edgings are used in a variety of ways:
Garters, anklets and wristlets, borders for robes, edging on clothing.

Medallion and Ladder Edging

MATERIALS
- 1 ball Lion Brand Recycled Cotton Yarn, Sand. 100g ball (169m/185yd)

NEEDLES
- US 8 (5 mm), large-eyed blunt needle for weaving in ends

SIZE
- To desired length

Instructions

Although it is not evident from the chart, the pattern actually produces a soft rounded edge.

Co 17 sts

R1 k1 k2tog yo k2 k5 k2tog yo k3 yo k2

R2 k2 yo k5 yo k2tog k4 k2tog yo k3

R3 k1 k2tog yo k2 k3 k2tog yo k1 k2tog yo k1 yo k2tog k1 yo k2

R4 k2 yo k1 k2tog yo k3 yo k2tog k1 yo k2tog k2 k2tog yo k3

R5 k1 k2tog yo k2 k1 k2tog yo k1 k2tog yo k5 yo k2tog k1 yo k2

R6 k2 yo k1 k2tog yo k3 yo k2tog k2 yo k2tog k1 yo k2 k2tog yo k3

R7 k1 k2tog yo k2 k3 k2tog k1 yo k2tog k3 k2tog yo k1 k2tog yo k1 k2tog

R8 bo 1 st, k1 yo k2tog k1 yo k2tog k1 k2tog yo k1 k2tog yo k3 k2tog yo k3

R9 k1 k2tog yo k2 k4 yo k2tog k1 yo, sl1 k2tog psso, yo k1 k2tog k1 k2tog

R10 k2 yo k2tog k3 k2tog yo k5 k2tog yo k3

R11 k1 k2tog yo k2 k6 yo k2tog k1 k2tog yo k3

R12 bo 2sts, k1 yo k3tog yo k7 k2tog yo k3

Repeat to desired length
Bo all st

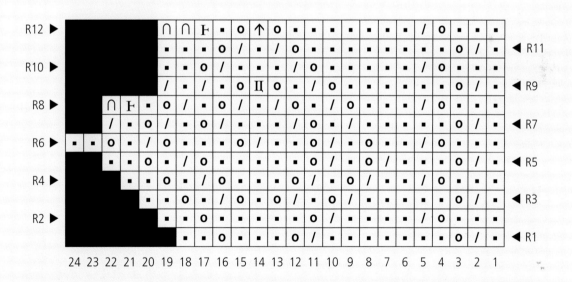

Scallop and Honeycomb Edging

MATERIALS
• 1 ball Caron Spa Acrylic and bamboo yarn, Rose Bisque. 85g ball (230m/251yds)

NEEDLES
• US 6 (4 mm), one US 7 (4.5 mm) for honeycomb bo, large-eyed blunt needle for weaving in ends

SIZE
• 5" x 5"

Instructions

The scallop edging is worked from side to side. The stitches for the honeycomb part are picked up from the straight edge and worked bottom to top. The honeycomb pattern used here is a variation of the four-row honeycomb pattern.

SCALLOP

Co 9 st loosely

Knit one row

R1 k2 yo k2tog yo k5

R2 slk k9

R3 k2 (yo k2tog) repeat ( ) one more time, yo k4

R4 slk k10

R5 k2 (yo k2tog) repeat ( ) two more times, yo k3

R6 slk k11

R7 k1 k2tog (yo k2tog) repeat ( ) two more times, k3

R8 slk k10

R9 k1 k2tog (yo k2tog) repeat ( ) one more time, k4

R10 slk k9

R11 k1 k2tog yo k2tog k5

R12 slk k8

Repeat R1-12 three more times

Bo all st loosely

Chart of Scallop

With straight edge and RS of work facing, pick up 26 sts evenly using a seed stitch pickup:

(k1 p1) repeat ( ) 12 more times

Next row: p1, k1 to end

HONEYCOMB VARIATION

R1 k1 (k2tog yo yo k2tog) repeat ( ) five more times, k1

R2 k1 (k1, k1 p1 into the yos, k1) repeat ( ) five more times, k1

R3 k1 k2 (k2tog yo yo k2tog) repeat ( ) four more times,   k2 k1

R4 k1 k2 (k1, k1 p1 into the yos, k1) repeat ( ) four more times, k2 k1

R5 (k1 p1) repeat ( ) twelve more times

R6 (p1 k1) repeat ( ) twelve more times

Repeat R1-R6 one more time

Repeat R1-R5 one more time

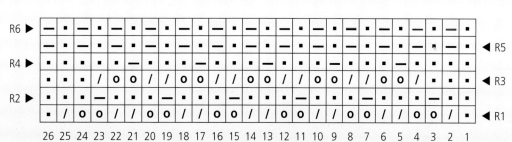

Chart of Honeycomb variation

Bo all st on wrong side using the US 7 (4.5 mm) needle (allows for a transition if picking up edging to continue on).

Pointed Edge, Eyelid and Holes Edging

MATERIALS
• 1 ball Lion Brand Recycled Cotton Yarn, Sand. 100g ball (169m/185yd)

NEEDLES
• Needles: US 8 (5 mm), one US 9 (5.5 mm) for bo, large-eyed blunt needle for weaving in ends

SIZE
• 5" x 5"

Instructions

POINTED EDGE

Co 5 sts loosely

R1 yo k2tog k3
R2 k2 yo k3
R3 yo k2tog k2 yo k2
R4 k3 yo k4
R5 yo k2tog k3 yo k3
R6 bo 4 sts, k4

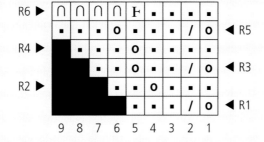

Repeat R1-R6 five more times
Bo all sts loosely

With RS of work facing, pick up 18 sts from the loops made by the yos.

Next row: k

EYELID

R1 k2 (k1 k2tog yo k1 yo k2tog k1) repeat ( )
one more time, k2

R2 k2 (k2tog yo k3 yo k2tog) repeat ( ) one
more time, k2

R3 k18

R4 k2 (k1 yo k2tog yo k3tog yo k1) repeat ( )
one more time, k2

R5 k18

R6 k2 (k2 yo k3tog yo k2) repeat ( ) one
more time, k2

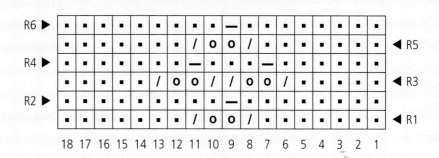

LACE HOLES

R1 k7 k2tog yo yo k2tog k7
R2 k8, k1 p1 into yos, k8
R3 k5 k2tog yo yo k2tog k2tog yo yo k2tog k5
R4 k6, k1 p1 into yos, k2, k1 p1 into yos, k6
R5 k7 k2tog yo yo k2tog k7
R6 k8, k1 p1 into yos, k8

Knit one row
Bo all sts using the US 9 (5.5 mm) needle

TECHNIQUE PRACTICE

1. Zig-Zag Practice
2. Lace Cable (page 26)
3. Ring Stitch Construction (page 27)
4. Face Cloths (pages 28-30)

• Technique practice is a good way of becoming familiar with patterns stitches. You can test for yarn shades and texture, and decide which colour shows the pattern in the best possible way before buying the yarn and committing to a larger piece.

• It is a place to do some experimentation: add rows of seed st, garter, Lace Holes or Vandyke to make an overall pattern more interesting.

• Combining different motifs or arranging motifs to make your own pattern is a lot of fun. Touch also play a role here: do the pattern stitches and yarn complement each other: e.g., pattern stitches look rugged but the piece is soft to the touch?

• Practice squares can become gift wraps; soft handmade face clothes are always welcomed. Face cloths can be used as gift wrapping: they can be made in a variety of beautiful colours and the content can be added depending on the occasion.

Zig-Zag Practice

MATERIALS
• small amount Patons Grace Yarn, Natural.   50g ball (125 m/ 136 yd)

NEEDLES
• US 6 (4 mm)

SIZE
• 3½" x 3½"

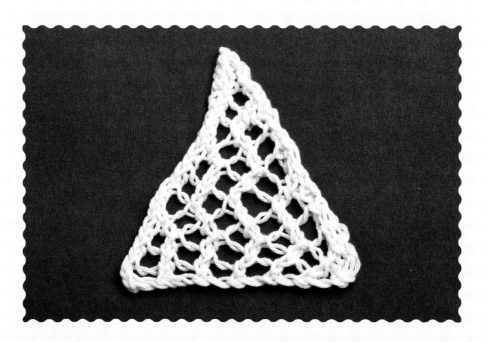

Instructions

This pattern produces a natural slant. Note that in the Circular shawl (page 116), even-numbered rows are k rather than p as it is worked in the round.

Co 16 sts

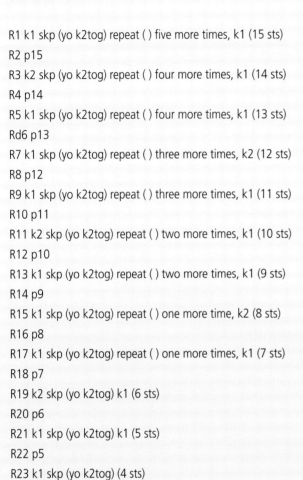

R1 k1 skp (yo k2tog) repeat ( ) five more times, k1 (15 sts)

R2 p15

R3 k2 skp (yo k2tog) repeat ( ) four more times, k1 (14 sts)

R4 p14

R5 k1 skp (yo k2tog) repeat ( ) four more times, k1 (13 sts)

Rd6 p13

R7 k1 skp (yo k2tog) repeat ( ) three more times, k2 (12 sts)

R8 p12

R9 k1 skp (yo k2tog) repeat ( ) three more times, k1 (11 sts)

R10 p11

R11 k2 skp (yo k2tog) repeat ( ) two more times, k1 (10 sts)

R12 p10

R13 k1 skp (yo k2tog) repeat ( ) two more times, k1 (9 sts)

R14 p9

R15 k1 skp (yo k2tog) repeat ( ) one more time, k2 (8 sts)

R16 p8

R17 k1 skp (yo k2tog) repeat ( ) one more time, k1 (7 sts)

R18 p7

R19 k2 skp (yo k2tog) k1 (6 sts)

R20 p6

R21 k1 skp (yo k2tog) k1 (5 sts)

R22 p5

R23 k1 skp (yo k2tog) (4 sts)

R24 p4

R25 k2tog k2tog

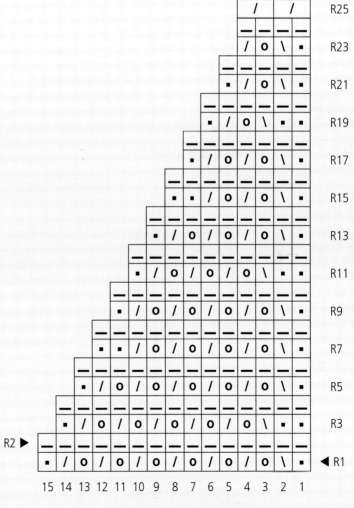

Chart showing the Zig-zag pattern

Lace Cable

MATERIALS

• 1 ball Lion Brand Recycled Cotton Yarn, Sand. 100g ball (169m/185yd)

NEEDLES

• Needles: US 8 (5 mm), US 9 (5.5 mm), size 8 cable needle, large-eyed blunt needle for weaving in ends

SIZE

• 5" (20 st) x 5½" (29 rows)

Instructions

The edging has a loose cast on to give loops at the beginning. The 4-st edges mirror each other with two seed stitches and two reverse stocking stitches. The last knit row on the larger needles and the bind off on the wrong side allows for ease of producing a seamless pick-up if you wish to continue with a different pattern to extend the edging with another pattern (returning to the smaller needles).

Cast on 20 st loosely

R1 k1 p1 p2 (k2tog yo k2) repeat ( ) two more times, p2 p1 k1

R2 k1 p1 k2 (p2tog yrn p2) repeat ( ) two more times, k2 p1 k1

R3-4 repeat R1, R2

R5-6 repeat R1, R2

R7 k1 p1 p2 k2tog yo k1, slip the next 3 sts onto cable needle and hold at back of work, k1 k2tog from left hand needle, yo, k2 from the cable needle, knit next st on left hand needle and last st on cable needle together, yo k2 p2 p1 k1

R8 repeat R2

R9-20 repeat R1, R2 six times

R21 repeat R7

R22 repeat R2

R23-28 repeat R1, R2 three times

Using needles one size larger (US 9, 5.5 mm) knit one row

Bo all st on the wrong side

Ring Stitch Construction

MATERIALS
- 1 ball Lion Brand Recycled Cotton Yarn, Sand. 100g ball (169m/185yd)

NEEDLES
- US 8 (5 mm), one US 9 (5.5 mm) for bo, large-eyed blunt needle for weaving in ends

SIZE
- 5" x 4½"

Instructions

The ring stitch pattern is 6 st +1. The pattern has 19 st of ring stitch plus a knit st at beginning and end of each row. The lace pattern is worked on every row and can be challenging. However, worked using this cotton and needle size, it gives good results. This pattern stitch is also sometimes known as Spider Stitch or Bird's Eye.

Co 21 sts firmly

R1 k1 k2 yo k3tog (yo k3 yo k3tog) repeat ( ) one more time, yo k2 k1

R2 k1 k1 (k2tog yo k1 yo k2tog k1) repeat ( ) two more times, k1

R3 k1 k1 k2tog (yo k1 yo k2tog yo k3tog) repeat ( ) one more time, yo k1 yo k2tog k1 k1

R4 k1 k1 (k2tog yo k1 yo k2tog k1) repeat ( ) two more times, k1

R5 k1 k2tog yo k3 yo (k3tog yo k3 yo) repeat ( ) one more time, k2tog k1

R6 k1 k1 (yo k2tog k1 k2tog yo k1) repeat ( ) two more times, k1

R7 k1 (k1 yo k2tog yo k3tog yo) repeat ( ) two more times, k1 k1

R8 k1 k1 (yo k2tog k1 k2tog yo k1) repeat ( ) two more times, k1

Repeat R1-R8 one more time
Repeat R1-R5 one more time

Bo all st on wrong side using the larger needle (allows for a transition if picking up edging to continue on).

Face Cloth Nº 1

MATERIALS
• 1 ball Lily Sugar'n Cream, Rose Pink. 113g ball (184m/200 yds)

NEEDLES
• US 9 (5.5 mm) needles

SIZE
• 9" x 7"

Instructions

This face cloth has a Seed Stitch border and Garter Stitch Circle Motif Center.

Co 35 sts firmly

BEGINNING
R1 (k1 p1) repeat ( ) 16 more times, k1

R2-R6 repeat R1

R7 k1 p1 k1 p1 k1 k25 k1 p1 k1 p1 k1

R8-R10 repeat R7

PATTERN
R1 k1 p1 k1 p1 k1 k2 (k1 k2togb yo k1 yo k2tog k1) repeat ( ) two more times, k2 k1 p1 k1 p1 k1

R2 k1 p1 k1 p1 k1 k25 k1 p1 k1 p1 k1

R3 k1 p1 k1 p1 k1 k2 (k2tog yo k3 yo k2tog) repeat ( ) two more times, k2 k1 p1 k1 p1 k1

R4 repeat R2

R5 k1 p1 k1 p1 k1 k2 (k1 yo k2tog k1 k2togb yo k1) repeat ( ) two more times, k2 k1 p1 k1 p1 k1

R6 repeat R2

R7 k1 p1 k1 p1 k1 k2 (k2 yo sskp yo k2) repeat ( ) two more times, k2 k1 p1 k1 p1 k1

R8 repeat R2

R9 k1 p1 k1 p1 k1 k9 k1 k2togb yo k1 yo k2tog k1 k9 k1 p1 k1 p1 k1

R10 repeat R2

R11 k1 p1 k1 p1 k1 k9 k2tog yo k3 yo k2tog k9 k1 p1 k1 p1 k1

R12 repeat R2

R13 k1 p1 k1 p1 k1 k9 k1 yo k2tog k1 k2togb yo k1 k9 k1 p1 k1 p1 k1

R14 repeat R2

R15 k1 p1 k1 p1 k1 k9 k2 yo sskp yo k2 k9 k1 p1 k1 p1 k1

R16 repeat R2

R17-R24 repeat R1-8 of the Pattern

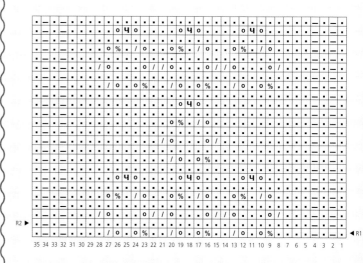

Chart of main section of pattern

FINISH
R1 k1 p1 k1 p1 k1 k25 k1 p1 k1 p1 k1

R2-R4 repeat R1

R5 (k1 p1) repeat ( ) 16 more times, k1

R6-R10 repeat R5

Bo all sts

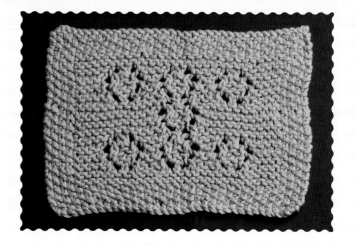

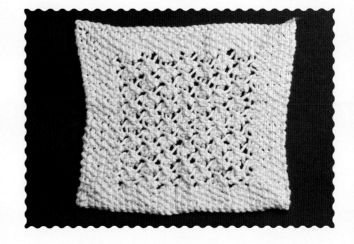

MATERIALS
- 1 ball Lily Sugar'n Cream, Yellow. 113g ball (184m/200 yds)

NEEDLES
- US 9 (5.5 mm) needles, needle for weaving in ends

SIZE
- 10" x 8"

Instructions

Pattern is worked with a 6-row seed st border at the beginning and end and the sides have a 5-st seed pattern.
The center section is Bead st. The four corners can be joined to make a small lace gift bag.

Co 35 sts

BORDER
R1 (k1 p1) repeat ( ) 16 more times, k1
R2-R6 repeat R1

Bead st (multiple of 6 +1 worked over four rows)

R7 k1 p1 k1 p1 k1 k2 (yo sskp yo k3) repeat ( ) two more times, yo sskp yo k2 k1 p1 k1 p1 k1
R8 k1 p1 k1 p1 k1 k1 (k2tog yo k1 yo k2tog k1) repeat ( ) three more times, k1 p1 k1 p1 k1
R9 k1 p1 k1 p1 k1 k2tog (yo k3 yo sskp) repeat ( ) two more times, yo k3 yo k2tog k1 p1 k1 p1 k1
R10 k1 p1 k1 p1 k1 k1 (yo k2tog k1 k2tog yo k1) repeat ( ) three more times, k1 p1 k1 p1 k1

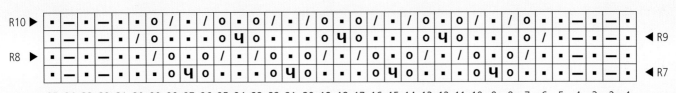

R11-R34 repeat R7-R10 six more times

BORDER
R35-R40 repeat R1 six more times

Bo all sts

Face Cloth № 3

MATERIALS
• 1 ball Lily Sugar'n Cream, Cornflower. 113g ball (184m/200 yds)

NEEDLES
• US 9 (5.5 mm) needles, needle for weaving in ends

SIZE
• 9" x 8"

Instructions

Pattern is worked with a 6-row seed st border at the beginning and end and the sides have a 5-st seed pattern. The center section is Ring st. The four corners can be joined to make a small lace gift bag.

Co 35 sts

BORDER
R1 (k1 p1) repeat ( ) 16 more times, k1
R2-R6 repeat R1

RING ST (MULTIPLE OF 6 +1 WORKED OVER EIGHT ROWS)
R7 k1 p1 k1 p1 k1 k2tog yo k3 yo (k3tog yo k3 yo) repeat ( ) two more times, k2tog k1 p1 k1 p1 k1
R8 k1 p1 k1 p1 k1 k1 (yo k2tog k1 k2tog yo k1) repeat ( ) three more times, k1 p1 k1 p1 k1
R9 k1 p1 k1 p1 k1 (k1 yo k2tog yo k3tog yo) repeat ( ) three more times, k1 k1 p1 k1 p1 k1
R10 k1 p1 k1 p1 k1 k1 (yo k2tog k1 k2tog yo k1) repeat ( ) three more times, k1 p1 k1 p1 k1
R11 k1 p1 k1 p1 k1 k2 yo k3tog (yo k3 yo k3tog) repeat ( ) two more times, yo k2 k1 p1 k1 p1 k1
R12 k1 p1 k1 p1 k1 k1 (k2tog yo k1 yo k2tog k1) repeat ( ) three more times k1 p1 k1 p1 k1
R13 k1 p1 k1 p1 k1 k1 k2tog (yo k1 yo k2tog yo k3tog) repeat ( ) two more times, yo k1 yo k2tog k1 k1 p1 k1 p1 k1
R14 k1 p1 k1 p1 k1 k1 (k2tog yo k1 yo k2tog k1) repeat ( ) three more times, k1 p1 k1 p1 k1

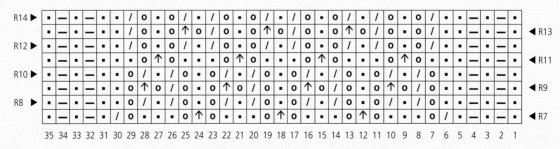

Chart of Ring st with 5-st seed pattern on each side

R15-R38 repeat R7-R14 three more times

BORDER
R39-R44 repeat R1 six more times
Bo all sts

Samplers

1. **Beginner Sampler**
2. **Heirloom Sampler (page 34)**

• Samplers are a good way of recording pattern stitches and understanding the construction of lace patterns.

• The beginner sampler allows a person new to lace knitting to see what is possible with some basic instructions. Spacing is important in lace knitting: it allows the overall pattern sts and motifs to stand on their own. The beginner lace sampler can be knitted in different colours to see the effect colour has on lace knitting.

• Intermediate lace and advanced lace samplers can involve loop and ladder edges and the patterns are chosen for placement to complement each other. Often an advanced lace sampler will be worked with lace on every row, many with eight different pattern sections or more. Some are worked in all garter stitch patterns and are the same when viewed from either side.

• An heirloom sampler is a piece which is often worked in very fine yarn and needles. They often include some family history or family interests in the selection of the motifs and patterns.

Beginner Sampler

MATERIALS
• 1 ball Lion Brand Recycled Cotton Yarn, Sand. 100g (169m/185yd) ball

NEEDLES
• US 9 (5.5 mm), large-eyed blunt needle for weaving in ends

SIZE
• 12" (67 rows) x 6" (23 sts)

Instructions

This sampler has been designed for a beginner, made in recycled cotton yarn. The lace is only worked on 26 rows so you have 42 rows of knits or purls. I have put the pattern together as a kind of walk through. I have explained each section and purpose. If you look closely at the centre leaf section you will see it has the Flower Motif in it. The Flower Motif can be used as a border or on a pocket. The leaf pattern can be put into a scarf. Knitting lace offers endless possibilities: looking at the construction of lace patterns helps you understand what is happening in your knitting. You can use any fibre of your choice - your yarn stash is an excellent place to begin. Light self colors are easier to knit with if you are new to lace knitting. One way to choose a needle size is look at what is recommended for the fibre and use needles one or two sizes larger.

Co 23 stitches firmly

R1 k

R2 k

___

R3-6 FLOWER STEM

R3 k1 (k1 k2tog yo k1 yo skp k1) repeat ( ) 2 more times, k1

R4 k1, p to last st, k1

R5 k1 (k2tog yo k3 yo skp) repeat ( ) 2 more times, k1

R6 k1, p to last st, k1

___

R7-8 SPACING

R7 k

R8 k1, p to last st, k1

___

R9-16 FLOWER

R9 k1 (k1 k2tog yo k1 yo skp k1) repeat ( ) 2 more times, k1

R10 k1, p to last st, k1

R11 k1 (k2tog yo k3 yo skp) repeat ( ) 2 more times, k1

R12 k1, p to last st, k1

R13 k1 (k1 yo skp k1 k2tog yo k1) repeat ( ) 2 more times, k1

R14 k1, p to last st, k1

R15 k1 (k2 yo, sl1 k2tog psso, yo k2) repeat ( ) 2 more times, k1

R16 k1 p to last st, k1

___

R17 SPACING

R17 k

___

EYELET RIDGE BEGINS

R18 k

___

EYELET ROW

R19 k1 (yo k2tog) repeat ( ) to end of row

___

EYELET RIDGE ENDS

R20 k

___

R21-22 SPACING

R21 k

R22 k1, p to last st, k1

R23-46 OVERALL LEAF PATTERN

2 st at beginning and end of row, multiple of 6st+1 (19 sts, total 23 sts) over 8 rows for total 24 rows

R23 k2 (k1 k2tog yo k1 yo skp) repeat ( ) two more times, k3

R24 k1, p to last st, k1

R25 k2 k2tog yo (k3 yo, sl1 k2tog psso, yo) repeat ( ) one more time, k3 yo k2tog k2

R26 k1, p to last st, k1

R27 k3 (yo skp k1 k2tog yo k1) repeat ( ) two more times, k2

R28 k1, p to last st, k1

R29 k4 (yo, sl1 k2tog psso, yo k3) repeat ( ) one more time, yo, sl1 k2tog psso, yo k4

R30 k1, p to last st, k1

R31-38 repeat 23-30

R39-46 repeat 23-30

___

R47 SPACING

R47 k

___

R48-52 COMPLETE EYELET RIDGE AND SPACING

Repeat R18-22

___

R53-65 FLOWER LEAVES AND FLOWER

Repeat R3-15

R66 k

R67 k

Bind off loosely, weave in ends of yarn, and block.

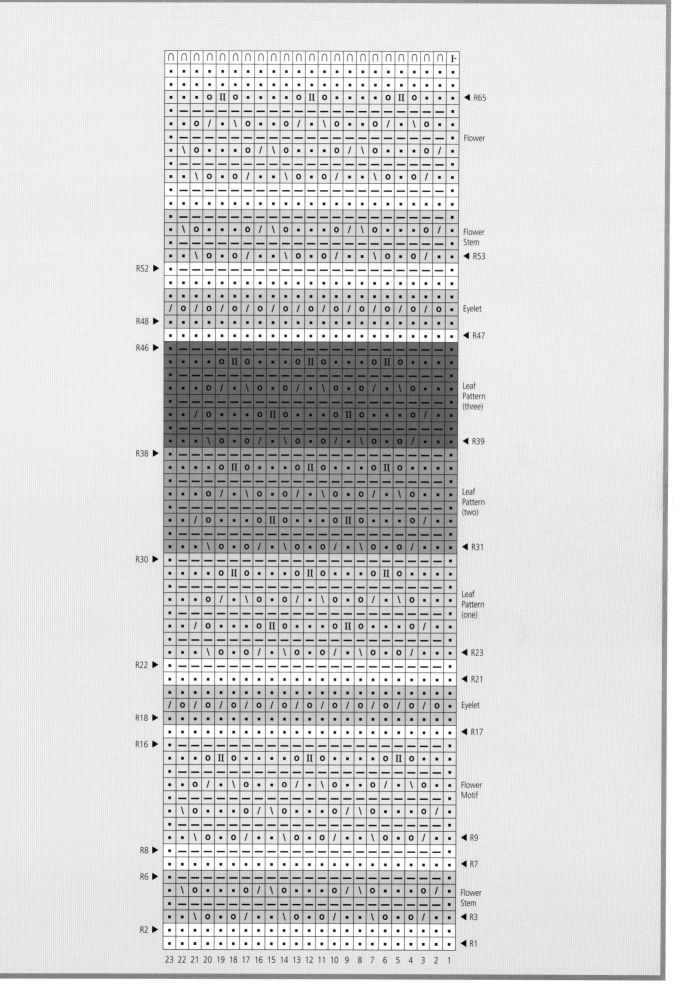

Heirloom Sampler

MATERIALS
• 60/2 silk thread, Natural

NEEDLES
• US 0 (2 mm)

SIZE
• 6" x 11"

Instructions

This heirloom sampler is an example of stitch placement, boldness and fragility, and a balance of solid and open work. Traditional stitches include Print of the Wave, Ring stitch, Honeycomb, and a Circle motif. Loop and Lace Ladder edgings as well as Lace holes and Eyelets have also been added.

Co 53 sts

R1-2 yo k2tog k1 yo k2tog, knit to last 5 sts, k1 yo k2tog k2

RING STITCH (R3-19)
R3 yo k2tog k1 yo k2tog k2 yo k3tog (yo k3 yo k3tog) repeat ( ) 5 more times, yo k2 k1 yo k2tog k2

R4 yo k2tog k1 yo k2tog k1 (k2tog yo k1 yo k2tog k1) repeat ( ) 6 more times, k1 yo k2tog k2

R5 yo k2tog k1 yo k2tog k1 k2tog (yo k1 yo k2tog yo k3tog) repeat ( ) 5 more times, yo k1 yo k2tog k1 k1 yo k2tog k2

R6 yo k2tog k1 yo k2tog k1 (k2tog yo k1 yo k2tog k1) repeat ( ) 6 more times, k1 yo k2tog k2

R7 yo k2tog k1 yo k2tog k2tog yo k3 yo (k3tog yo k3 yo) repeat ( ) 5 more times, k2tog k1 yo k2tog k2

R8 yo k2tog k1 yo k2tog k1 (yo k2tog k1 k2tog yo k1) repeat ( ) 6 more times, k1 yo k2tog k2

R9 yo k2tog k1 yo k2tog (k1 yo k2tog yo k3tog yo) repeat ( ) 6 more times, k1 k1 yo k2tog k2

R10 yo k2tog k1 yo k2tog k1 (yo k2tog k1 k2tog yo k1) repeat ( ) 6 more times, k1 yo k2tog k2

R11-18 repeat rows 3-10 one more time

R19 repeat R3 one more time

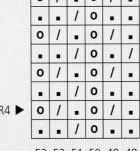
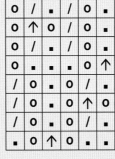
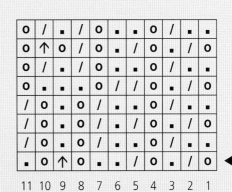

R4 ▶ (on left chart)

◀ R3 (on right chart)

53 52 51 50 49 48   repeat over 36 sts   11 10 9 8 7 6 5 4 3 2 1

Chart of Ring stitch

SEPARATION ROWS (R20-22)

R20-22 yo k2tog k1 yo k2tog, k to last 5 sts, k1 yo k2tog k2

EYELET (R23-24)

R23 yo k2tog k1 yo k2tog k1 (yo k2tog) repeat ( ) 20 more times, k1 yo k2tog k2
R24 yo k2tog k1 yo k2tog, k to last 5 sts, k1 yo k2tog k2

SEPARATION ROWS (R25-26)

R25-26 yo k2tog k1 yo k2tog, k to last 5 sts, k1 yo k2tog k2

CIRCLE MOTIF (R27-34)

R27 yo k2tog k1 yo k2tog k2 (k1 k2tog yo k1 yo k2togb k2) repeat ( ) 4 more times, k1 k1 yo k2tog k2
R28 yo k2tog k1 yo k2tog, k to last 5 sts, k1 yo k2tog k2
R29 yo k2tog k1 yo k2tog k2 (k2tog yo k3 yo k2tog k1) repeat ( ) 4 more times, k1 k1 yo k2tog k2
R30 yo k2tog k1 yo k2tog, k to last 5 sts k1 yo k2tog k2
R31 yo k2tog k1 yo k2tog k2 (k1 yo k2togb k1 k2tog yo k2) repeat ( ) 4 more times, k1 k1 yo k2tog k2
R32 yo k2tog k1 yo k2tog, k to last 5 sts, k1 yo k2tog k2
R33 yo k2tog k1 yo k2tog k2 (k2 yo k3tog yo k3) repeat ( ) 4 more times, k1 k1 yo k2tog k2
R34 yo k2tog k1 yo k2tog, k to last 5 sts k1 yo k2tog k2

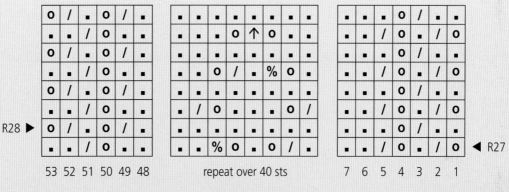

53 52 51 50 49 48   repeat over 40 sts   7 6 5 4 3 2 1

Chart of Circle Motif

SEPARATION ROWS (R35-36)

R35-36 yo k2tog k1 yo k2tog, k to last 5 sts, k1 yo k2tog k2

EYELET (R37-38)

R37 yo k2tog k1 yo k2tog k1 (yo k2tog) repeat ( ) 20 more times, k1 yo k2tog k2
R38 yo k2tog k1 yo k2tog, k to last 5 sts, k1 yo k2tog k2

SEPARATION ROWS (R39-40)

R39-40 yo k2tog k1 yo k2tog, k to last 5 sts, k1 yo k2tog k2

PRINT OF THE WAVE WITH LACE HOLES (R41-100)

R41 yo k2tog k1 yo k2tog k8 k3 k2tog yo k2tog yo k2tog yo k1 k2tog k3 k2tog k1 yo k1 yo k2tog yo k2tog yo k4 k8 k1 yo k2tog k2

R42 yo k2tog k1 yo k2tog, k to last 5 sts, k1 yo k2tog k2

R43 yo k2tog k1 yo k2tog k2 k2tog yo yo k2tog k2 k3 k2tog yo k2tog yo k2tog yo k1 k2tog k1 k2tog k1 yo k3 yo k2tog yo k2tog yo k4 k2 k2tog yo yo k2tog k2 k1 yo k2tog k2

R44 yo k2tog k1 yo k2tog k4 p1 k3 k27 k4 p1 k3 k1 yo k2tog k2

R45 yo k2tog k1 yo k2tog k8 k3 k2tog yo k2tog yo k2tog yo k1, s11 k2tog psso, k1 yo k5 yo k2tog yo k2tog yo k4 k8 k1 yo k2tog k2

R46 yo k2tog k1 yo k2tog, k to last 5 sts, k1 yo k2tog k2

R47 yo k2tog k1 yo k2tog k8 k4 yo k2tog yo k2tog yo k1 k1 k2tog k3 k2tog k1 yo k2tog yo k2tog yo k2tog k3 k8 k1 yo k2tog k2

R48 yo k2tog k1 yo k2tog, k to last 5 sts, k1 yo k2tog k2

R49 yo k2tog k1 yo k2tog k4 k2tog yo yo k2tog k4 k2tog yo k2tog yo k3 yo k1 k2tog k1 k2tog k1 yo k2tog yo k2tog yo k2tog k3 k2tog yo yo k2tog k4 k1 yo k2tog k2

R50 yo k2tog k1 yo k2tog k6 p1 k1 k27 k2 p1 k5 k1 yo k2tog k2

R51 yo k2tog k1 yo k2tog k8 k4 yo k2tog yo k2tog yo k5 yo k1, s11 k2tog psso, k1 yo k2tog yo k2tog yo k2tog k3 k8 k1 yo k2tog k2

R52 yo k2tog k1 yo k2tog, k to last 5 sts, k1 yo k2tog k2

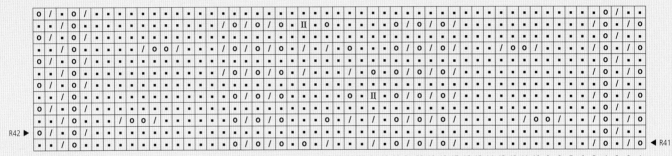

Chart of Print of the Wave with Lace Holes

R53-100 repeat R41-52 four more times

SEPARATION ROWS (R101-102)

R101-102 yo k2tog k1 yo k2tog, k to last 5 sts, k1 yo k2tog k2

EYELET (R103-104)

R103 yo k2tog k1 yo k2tog k1 (yo k2tog) repeat ( ) 20 more times, k1 yo k2tog k2

R104 yo k2tog k1 yo k2tog, k to last 5 sts, k1 yo k2tog k2

SEPARATION ROWS (R105-106)

R105-106 yo k2tog k1 yo k2tog, k to last 5 sts, k1 yo k2tog k2

CIRCLE MOTIF (R107-114)

R107 yo k2tog k1 yo k2tog, k2, (k1 k2tog, yo k1 yo k2togb k2) repeat ( ) 4 more times, k1 k1 yo k2tog k2

R108 yo k2tog k1 yo k2tog, k to last 5 sts, k1 yo k2tog k2

R109 yo k2tog k1 yo k2tog k2 (k2tog yo k3 yo k2tog k1) repeat ( ) 4 more times, k1 k1 yo k2tog k2

R110 yo k2tog k1 yo k2tog, k to last 5 sts, k1 yo k2tog k2

R111 yo k2tog k1 yo k2tog k2 (k1 yo k2togb k1 k2tog yo k2) repeat ( ) 4 more times, k1 k1 yo k2tog k2

R112 yo k2tog k1 yo k2tog, k to last 5 sts, k1 yo k2tog k2

R113 yo k2tog k1 yo k2tog k2 (k2 yo k3tog yo k3) repeat ( ) 4 more times, k1 k1 yo k2tog k2

R114 yo k2tog k1 yo k2tog, k to last 5 sts, k1 yo k2tog k2

SEPARATION ROWS (R115-116)

R115-116 yo k2tog k1 yo k2tog, k to last 5 sts, k1 yo k2tog k2 [increase]

EYELET (R117-118)

R117 yo k2tog k1 yo k2tog k1 (yo k2tog) repeat ( ) 20 more times, k1 yo k2tog k2

R118 yo k2tog k1 yo k2tog, k to last 5 sts, k1 yo k2tog k2

SEPARATION ROWS (R119-120)

R119 yo k2tog k1 yo k2tog, k to last 5 sts, k1 yo k2tog k2

R120 yo k2tog k1 yo k2tog, k to last 6 sts, increase on next stitch, k1 yo k2tog k2 (54 sts)

HONEYCOMB (R121-136) (54 STS)

R121 yo k2tog k1 yo k2tog (k2tog yo yo k2tog) repeat ( ) 10 more times, k1 yo k2tog k2

R122 yo k2tog k1 yo k2tog (k2 p1 k1) repeat ( ) 10 more times, k1 yo k2tog k2

R123 yo k2tog k1 yo k2tog k2 (k2tog yo yo k2tog) repeat ( ) 9 more times, k2 k1 yo k2tog k2

R124 yo k2tog k1 yo k2tog k2 (k2 p1 k1) repeat ( ) 9 more times, k2 k1 yo k2tog k2

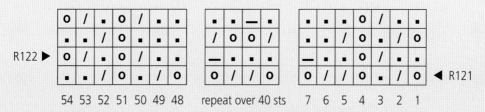

Chart of Honeycomb. This section has 54 sts, using the extra stitch made on R120

R125-136 repeat R121-124 three more times

R137-138 yo k2tog k1 yo k2tog, knit to last 5 sts, k1 yo k2tog k2
Bo all sts loosely

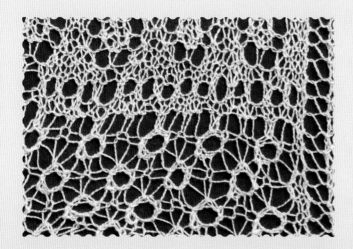
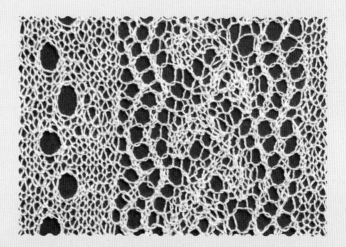

ACCESSORIES

Accessories come into two categories: functional-wearable and decorative-wearable. Both categories are easy to knit.
The possibilities are endless and I use yarn left over from other projects. Lots of creative ideas come from making these accessories.

Loops and Ladder Necklace

MATERIALS
• 1 ball SAX Ornaghi filati yarn, Royal Blue. 20g ball (140m/160yds)

NEEDLES
• US 2 (2.75 mm) needles. Small button or bead to close. Sewing needle to weave in ends

SIZE
• 1.4" x 21.7" (slightly stretchy)

Instructions

Special Notes The pattern is worked with short rows to form a curve
• Section 1: 7sts 4 row repeats with 1 short row
• Section 2: 7sts 8 row repeats with 1 short row
• Section 3: 7sts 4 row repeats with 1 short row

Cast on 7 sts loosely.
Knit 2 rows

SECTION 1
R1 k3 yo k2tog yo yo k1 yo yo k1
R2 k1, k1 p1 into yos, k1, k1 p1 into yos, k1 yo k2tog turn
R3 k1 yo k2tog k6
R4 bo 4sts, k2 yo k2tog k2

Work 20 more sections

SECTION 2

R1 k3 yo k2tog yo yo k1 yo yo k1

R2 k1, k1 p1 into yos, k1, k1 p1 into yos, k1 yo k2tog k2

R3 k3 yo k2tog k6

R4 bo 4sts, k1 k1 yo k2tog turn

R5 k1 yo k2tog yo yo k1 yo yo k1

R6 k1, k1 p1 into yos, k1, k1 p1 into yos, k1 yo k2tog k2

R7 k3 yo k2tog k6

R8 bo 4sts, k2 yo k2tog k2

Work 7 more sections

SECTION 3 (Same as Section 1)

Knit 2 rows

Bo loosely

Finish off by weaving in threads and sew a small button or bead to one end, a small loop to the other end to close.

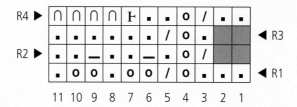

One 4-row repeat from sections 1 and 3

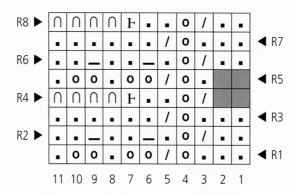

One 8-row repeat from section 2

Lace Leaves

Knitted with small amounts of various left-over yarns.

Instructions

PATTERN 1: LACE LADDER (A THREE-STITCH LADDER)

Co 2 sts

Knit 2 sts

R1 yo k2

R2 yo k3

R3 yo k4

R4 yo k5

R5 yo k6 (7 sts)

R6 yo k2 (k1 yo k2tog) k2

R7 yo k2 (k1 yo k2tog) k3

R8 yo k3 (k1 yo k2tog) k3

R9 yo k3 (k1 yo k2tog) k4

R10 yo k4 (k1 yo k2tog) k4

R11 yo k4 (k1 yo k2tog) k5 (13 sts)

R12 yo k2 (k1 yo k2tog) repeat ( ) two more times, k2

R13 yo k2 (k1 yo k2tog) repeat ( ) two more times, k3

R14 yo k3 (k1 yo k2tog) repeat ( ) two more times, k3

R15 yo k3 (k1 yo k2tog) repeat ( ) two more times, k4

R16 yo k4 (k1 yo k2tog) repeat ( ) two more times, k4

R17 yo k4 (k1 yo k2tog) repeat ( ) two more times, k5

R18 yo k2 (k1 yo k2tog) repeat ( ) four more times, k2

R19 yo k2 (k1 yo k2tog) repeat ( ) four more times, k3 (21 sts)

R20 (k3tog) repeat ( ) six more times

R21 k3tog k1 k3tog

R22 bo all sts

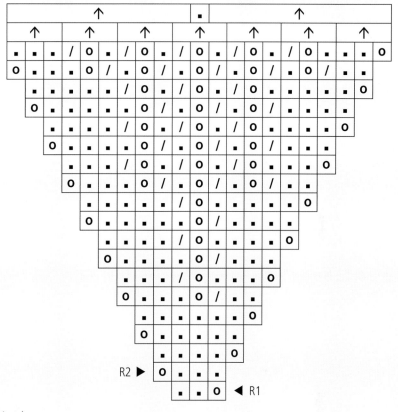

Chart of Lace Ladder pattern

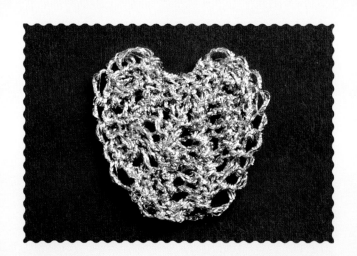

PATTERN 2: HOLE LADDER (A FOUR-STITCH LADDER)

Co 2 sts

Knit 2 sts

R1 yo k2

R2 yo k3

R3 yo k4

R4 yo k5

R5 yo k6

R6 yo k7 (8 sts)

R7 yo k2 (k2tog yo yo k2tog) k2

R8 yo k2 (k1, k1 p1 into yos, k1) k3

R9 yo k3 (k2tog yo yo k2tog) k3

R10 yo k3 (k1, k1 p1 into yos, k1) k4

R11 yo k4 (k2tog yo yo k2tog) k4

R12 yo k4 (k1, k1 p1 into yos, k1) k5

R13 yo k5 (k2tog yo yo k2tog) k5

R14 yo k5 (k1, k1 p1 into yos, k1) k6 (16 sts)

R15 yo k2 (k2tog yo yo k2tog) repeat ( ) two more times, k2

R16 yo k2 (k1, k1 p1 into yos, k1) repeat ( ) two more times, k3

R17 yo k3 (k2tog yo yo k2tog) repeat ( ) two more times, k3

R18 yo k3 (k1, k1 p1 into yos, k1) repeat ( ) two more times, k4

R19 yo k4 (k2tog yo yo k2tog) repeat ( ) two more times, k4

R20 yo k4 (k1, k1 p1 into yos, k1) repeat ( ) two more times, k5

R21 yo k1 (k2tog yo yo k2tog) repeat ( ) four more times, k1

R22 yo k1 (k1, k1 p1 into yos, k1) repeat ( ) four more times, k2 (24 sts)

R23 (k3tog) repeat ( ) seven more times

R24 k3tog k2 k3tog

R25 bo all st

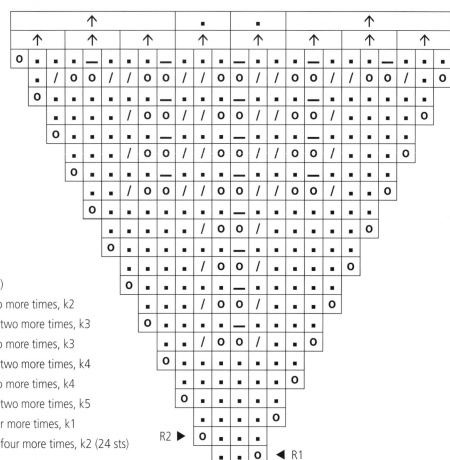

Chart of Hole Ladder pattern

PATTERN 3: CIRCLE MOTIF (A SEVEN-STITCH MOTIF)

Co 2 sts

Knit 2 sts

R1 yo k2

R2 yo k3

R3 yo k4

R4 yo k5

R5 yo k6

R6 yo k7

R7 yo k8

R8 yo k9

R9 yo k10 (11 sts)

R10 yo k2 (k1 k2tog yo k1 yo k2tog k1) k2

R11 yo k12

R12 yo k3 (k2tog yo k3 yo k2tog) k3

R13 yo k14

R14 yo k4 (k1 yo k2tog k1 k2tog yo k1) k4

R15 yo k16

R16 yo k5 (k2 yo k3tog yo k2) k5 (18 sts)

R17 yo k18

R18 yo k19

R19 yo k20

R20 yo k21

R21 yo k22 (23 sts)

R22 k1 (k3tog) repeat ( ) six more times, k1

R23 k3tog k3tog k3tog

R24 bo all sts

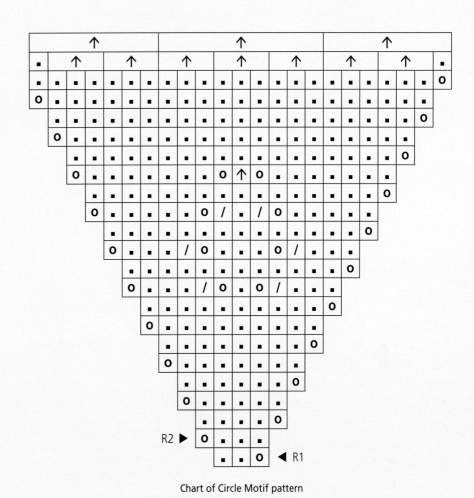

Chart of Circle Motif pattern

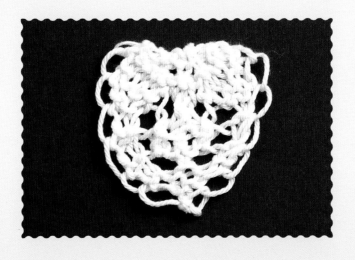

Fine Lace Garter

MATERIALS
• Small amount of Habu Silk and Stainless Steel yarn

NEEDLES
• US 0 (2 mm)

SIZE
• 14" circumference x 2½"

Instructions

Garters are fun to make. They can be simple or complex. Basically they are edgings with eyelet holes for elastic and ribbon. There are many variations and the results are satisfying. They can be designed to be worn above the knee, below the knee or around one ankle.

Co 12 sts
Knit two rows

R1 k3 yo k2tog k2 yo k2tog yo k1 yo k2

R2 yo k2tog k5 yo k2tog k5

R3 k5 2 yo k2tog yo k3 yo k2

R4 yo k2tog k7 yo k2tog k5

R5 k5 2 yo k2tog yo k1 yo, sl1 k2tog psso, yo k1 yo k2

R6 yo k2tog k9 yo k2tog k5

R7 k5 2 yo k2tog yo k3 yo k1 yo k3 yo k2

R8 yo k2tog k13 yo k2tog k5

R9 k3 yo k2tog k2 (yo, sl1 k2tog psso) repeat ( ) one more time, yo k3 yo, sl1 k2tog psso, yo k2tog k1

R10 yo k2tog k11 yo k2tog k5

R11 k5 2 yo, sl1 k2tog psso, k2tog (yo, sl1 k2tog psso) repeat ( ) one more time, k2tog

R12 yo k2tog k6 yo k2tog k5

R13 k5 2 (yo, sl1 k2tog psso) repeat ( ) one more time, k2tog

R14 yo k2tog k3 yo k2tog k5

Repeat R1-R14 to desired length

Knit two rows
Bo all sts

Chart of pattern showing placement of holes for elastic and ribbon on sts 4 and 5 of R1 and R9

Row labels (left): R14, R12, R10, R8, R6, R4, R2
Row labels (right): R13, R11, R9, R7, R5, R3, R1
Column numbers: 22 21 20 19 18 17 16 15 14 13 12 11 10 9 8 7 6 5 4 3 2 1

Boot Toppers

MATERIALS
• One ball Patons Stretch Socks Yarn, Marshmallow. 50g ball (219 m/ 239 yd)

NEEDLES
• Four double-pointed US 5 (3.75 mm) needles, blunt ended needle for weaving ends

SIZE
• Bottom circumference 12" (slightly stretchy), top circumference 10" (slightly stretchy), bottom-top 5"

Instructions

Knitted in rounds (Rd). The pattern is in multiples of 8 sts. To make smaller or larger circumference, reduce or increase in multiples of eight.

Co 88 sts firmly

Divide onto three needles as follows: 24 sts, 32 sts, 32 sts

Rd1 (k2tog yo yo k2tog p4) repeat ( ) 10 more times
Rd2 (k1, k1 p1 into yos, k1 p4) repeat ( ) 10 more times
Rd3 (k4 p2tog yrn yrn p2tog) repeat ( ) 10 more times
Rd4 (k4 p1, k1 p1 into yos, p1) repeat ( ) 10 more times

repeat over 88 sts

Chart of Pattern Repeat

Repeat Rd1-Rd4 seven more times

DECREASE ROUND
(k9 k2tog) repeat ( ) 7 more times (80 sts)

Knit three rounds

RIB
Change to (k1 p1) rib, work 16 rounds
Bo in rib, weave in loose ends

Knit second boot topper

Anklets

MATERIALS
• One ball Patons Stretch Socks Yarn, Black Taffy. 50g ball (219 m / 239 yd). Elastic

NEEDLES
• US 3 (3.25 mm), US 1 (2.25 mm)

SIZE
• 8" circumference x 4" (plus 1" turnover)

Instructions

Co 17 sts using US 3 needles

R1 k1 k2tog yo k2 k5 k2tog yo k3 yo k2

R2 k2 yo k5 yo k2tog k4 k2tog yo k3

R3 k1 k2tog yo k2 k3 k2tog yo k1 k2tog yo k1 yo k2tog k1 yo k2

R4 k2 yo k1 k2tog yo k3 yo k2tog k1 yo k2tog k2 k2tog yo k3

R5 k1 k2tog yo k2 k1 k2tog yo k1 k2tog yo k5 yo k2tog k1 yo k2

R6 k2 yo k1 k2tog yo k3 yo k2tog k2 yo k2tog k1 yo k2 k2tog yo k3

R7 k1 k2tog yo k2 k3 k2tog k1 yo k2tog k3 k2tog yo k1 k2tog yo k1 k2tog

R8 bo 1 st, k1 yo k2tog k1 yo k2tog k1 k2tog yo k1 k2tog yo k3 k2tog yo k3

R9 k1 k2tog yo k2 k4 yo k2tog k1 yo sl1 k2tog psso yo k1 k2tog k1 k2tog

R10 k2 yo k2tog k3 k2tog yo k5 k2tog yo k3

R11 k1 k2tog yo k2 k6 yo k2tog k1 k2tog yo k3

R12 bo 2sts, k1 yo k3tog yo k7 k2tog yo k3

Repeat six more times
Bo all st

Change to US 1 needles
With RS and straight edge facing, pick up 90 sts along the straight edge.

RIB
R1 k3 (p2 k2) repeat to last three sts, p3
Repeat R1 17 more times

Bo all sts

Sew seams from straight edge to 1" from scallop edge to leave an indentation for the back of the ankle

Cut a piece of elastic about 1" shorter than the circumference, place inside rib, fold edge over and sew on inside

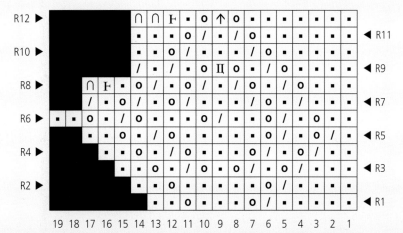

Chart of pattern stitches. Although it is not evident from the chart, the pattern actually produces a soft rounded edge

BABY WEAR

Lace is often found in baby-wear knitting. Very often small motifs or short repeat rows are used. Baby wear items are small and the small pattern sts and motif sizes often reflect the length and width of the knitting. Traditional lace baby wear was knitted in fine yarns and needles, but today all types of yarns and needles are used.

Newborn Baby Bonnet

MATERIALS
• 1 ball Patons Grace Yarn, Amethyst. 50g ball (125m/136yds)

NEEDLES
• US 6 (4 mm), needle for weaving ends

SIZE
• 12" circumference, height 5½"

Instructions

BONNET EDGING
Co 4 sts loosely

Knit one row

R1 k4

R2 k2 yo k2

R3 k3 yo k2

R4 k3 yo k3

R5 k4 yo k3

R6 bo 4 sts, k3

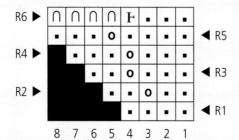

Repeat R1-R6 16 more times

Bo loosely

With RS facing pick up 53 sts along the straight edge

Next row: knit

(continued on page 52)

50

(continued from page 50)

RING STITCH (MULTIPLES OF 6+1) PLUS A LOOP AT EACH END

There are two stitches worked at the beginning of each row with a yo k2tog to make a loop edging along the main section of the bonnet. On the return row they are worked as k2.

R1 yo k2tog k2tog yo k3 yo (k3tog yo k3 yo) repeat ( ) six more times, k2tog k2

R2 yo k2tog k1 (yo k2tog k1 k2tog yo k1) repeat ( ) seven more times, k2

R3 yo k2tog (k1 yo k2tog yo k3tog yo) repeat ( ) seven more times, k1 k2

R4 yo k2tog k1 (yo k2tog k1 k2tog yo k1) repeat ( ) seven more times, k2

R5 yo k2tog k2 yo k3tog (yo k3 yo k3tog) repeat ( ) six more times, yo k2 k2

R6 yo k2tog k1 (k2tog yo k1 yo k2tog k1) repeat ( ) seven more times, k2

R7 yo k2tog k1 k2tog (yo k1 yo k2tog yo k3tog) repeat ( ) six more times, yo k1 yo k2tog k1 k2

R8 yo k2tog k1 (k2tog yo k1 yo k2tog k1) repeat ( ) seven more times, k2

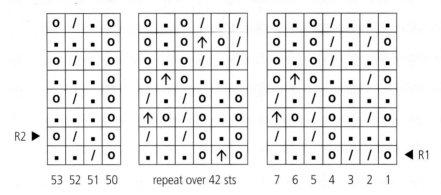

53 52 51 50   repeat over 42 sts   7 6 5 4 3 2 1

Chart of Ring stitch

Repeat R1-R8 one more time

Repeat R1-R4 one more time

DECREASE FOR CROWN

R1 k26 k2tog k25 (52 sts)

R2 k52

R3 k2 (k4 k2tog) repeat ( ) seven more times, k2 (44 sts)

R4 k44

R5 k2 (k3 k2tog) repeat ( ) seven more times, k2 (36 sts)

R6 k36

R7 k2 (k2 k2tog) repeat ( ) seven more times, k2 (28 sts)

R8 k28

R9 k2 (k1 k2tog) repeat ( ) seven more times, k2 (20 sts)

R10 k20

R11 k2 (k2tog) repeat ( ) seven more times, k2 (12 sts)

R12 k12

R13 (k2tog) repeat ( ) five more times (6 sts)

Thread yarn through remaining sts firmly and sew a seam from the center crown to the beginning of decreases.

Toddler Hat

MATERIALS
• 1 ball Patons Grace Yarn, Rosewood. 50g ball (125m/136yds)

NEEDLES
• US 6 (4 mm), US 2 (3 mm)

SIZE
• 18" inside brim circumference, 5" from inside brim to crown

Instructions

Co 140 sts

SEED STITCH AND HONEYCOMB BRIM
R1 (k1 p1) repeat ( ) to end of row

R2 (p1 k1) repeat ( ) to end of row

R3 repeat R1

R4 repeat R2

R5 (k2tog yo yo k2tog) repeat ( ) to end of row

R6 (k1, k1 p1 into yos, k1) repeat ( ) repeat ( ) to end of row

R7 k2 (k2tog yo yo k2tog) repeat ( ) to last 2 sts, k2

R8 k2 (k1, k1 p1 into yos, k1) repeat ( ) to last 2 sts, k2

R9 repeat R5

R10 repeat R6

R11 repeat R1

R12 repeat R2

Change to US 2 needles

DECREASE ROWS
R13 (p2tog) repeat ( ) to end of row (70 sts RS)

R14 k2tog, k to last 2 sts, k2tog (68 sts WS)

Change back to US 6 needles

24 ROWS OF LEAF STITCH PATTERN
Multiples of 6 sts +1, with an extra st at the beginning of the RS rows and end of WS rows

R1 k1 (k1 k2tog yo k1 yo k2togb) repeat ( ) to last st, k1

R2 p

R3 k1 k2tog yo (k3 yo sskp yo) repeat ( ) to last 5 sts, k3 yo k2tog

R4 p

Chart of Seed Stitch and Honeycomb Brim

R5 k1 k1 (yo k2ogb k1 k2tog yo k1) repeat ( ) to end of row

R6 p

R7 k1 k2 (yo sskp yo k3) repeat ( ) to last 5 sts, yo sskp yo k2

R8 p

Repeat R1-R8 two more times

Next row: k

Next row: p (68 sts)

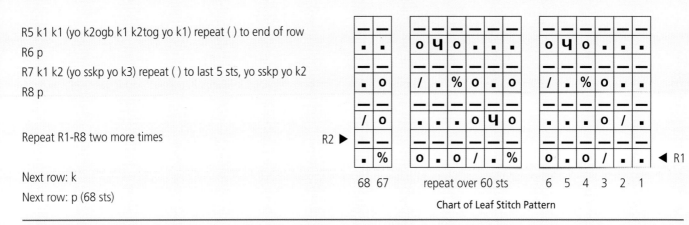

Chart of Leaf Stitch Pattern

DECREASE FOR CROWN

R1 k1 (skp k7 k2tog) repeat ( ) 5 more times, k1 (56 sts)

R2 and every alternate row to R12: p

R3 k

R5 k1 (skp k5 k2tog) repeat ( ) 5 more times, k1 (44 sts)

R7 k

R9 k1 (skp k3 k2tog) repeat ( ) 5 more times, k1 (32 sts)

R11 k1 (skp k1 k2tog) repeat ( ) 5 more times, k1 (20 sts)

R13 (k2tog) repeat ( ) 9 more times (10 sts)

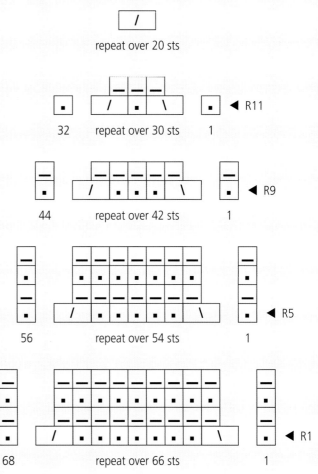

Chart showing the pattern of decreases within this section. Each skp and k2tog reduces the number of sts on the row by 1

Thread yarn through the remaining stitches, sew up the seam, leaving the brim ends open to overlap slightly.

"Celebration" Baby Robe

MATERIALS
• Six balls Patons Grace Yarn, Natural. 50g ball (125 m/ 136 yd)

NEEDLES
• US 6 (4 mm), US 4 (3.5 mm), blunt ended needle for weaving in ends, small button

SIZE
• Length 31", chest 18", for newborn

Instructions

This robe is made from a trim, border, main part, bodice and cuffs. The trim begins with a yo k2tog which forms a loop on every alternate row. These loops then become stitches to be picked up for the border section. It provides an eyelet-type row and is simpler than trying to evenly pick up stitches along the straight edge.

SEAMS
The 5-st loop and ladder at the beginning and end of each row are used to make a lace seam, described in the Techniques section. The approach is a loop-weave seam, which only involves the actual loops and a crochet hook. If you are thinking of using this method, try a test piece of the loop-weaving before beginning the robe.

Alternatively, the Kitchener stitch or grafting method can be used using the loops as stitches. Another approach is to replace the (yo k2tog) at the beginning and end of each row with a k1 p1 seed st at the beginning and p1 k1 at the end of the row and sew up the seam; you will still have the 3-st lace ladder after the seed st.

BACK

TRIM
US 6 (4mm) Co 8 sts firmly

Knit one row

R1 yo k2tog k1 yo k2tog k1 yo yo k2
R2 slk k1 k1 p1 k1 k1 yo k2tog k2
R3 yo k2tog k1 yo k2tog k3 k2tog
R4 bo 1 st, k2 k1 yo k2tog k2

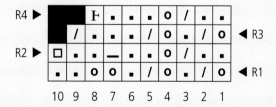

Repeat R1-R4 41 more times

Last row:
Yo, k2tog k to end of row
Bo all sts firmly

BORDER

With RS facing, starting at the bo edge, run the needle through the back of the loops picking up 85 sts. Join yarn.

Separation row:

yo k2tog k1 yo k2tog k75 k1 yo k2tog k2

A 5-st loop and ladder edging, yo k2tog k1 yo k2tog, at the beginning, and k1 yo k2tog k2 at the end of each row is now in place. The 75 sts in the middle are worked as follows: 1 k st at each end and 73 sts of Bead Stitch, which is multiples of 6 st +1 worked over 4 rows.

Pattern:

Bead Stitch

R1 yo k2tog k1 yo k2tog k1 k2 (yo sskp yo k3) repeat ( ) 10 more times, yo sskp yo k2 k1 k1 yo k2tog k2
R2 yo k2tog k1 yo k2tog k1 k1 (k2tog yo k1 yo k2tog k1) repeat ( ) 11 more times, k1 k1 yo k2tog k2
R3 yo k2tog k1 yo k2tog k1 k2tog (yo k3 yo sskp) repeat ( ) 10 more times, yo k3 yo k2tog k1 k1 yo k2tog k2
R4 yo k2tog k1 yo k2tog k1 k1 (yo k2tog k1 k2tog yo k1) repeat ( ) 11 more times, k1 k1 yo k2tog k2

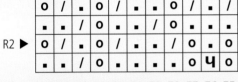

85 84 83 82 81 80 79 78 77 76 75

repeat over 60 sts

14 13 12 11 10 9 8 7 6 5 4 3 2 1

Chart of Bead Stitch

Repeat R1-R4 three more times
Repeat R1-R3 one more time

Separation rows:

Next row: yo k2tog k1 yo k2tog k75 k1 yo k2tog k2
Repeat this row two more times

EYELET ROWS

R1 yo k2tog k1 yo k2tog (k2tog yo) repeat ( ) 36 more times, k1 k1 yo k2tog k2
R2 yo k2tog k1 yo k2tog k75 k1 yo k2tog k2

MAIN PART

This section is worked continuing the 5-st loop and ladder at the beginning (place st marker), a 17 st panel (place st marker), then there are 41 sts of Print-of-the-Wave panel (place st marker), another 17 st panel (place st marker), and a 5-st ladder and loop at the end. The Print-of-the-Wave is a 12 row repeat. The Lace Holes are on 17-st side panels worked over 12 rows, with the holes on rows 3, 4, 9 and 10, on every alternate 12-row section.

Print of the wave with lace holes:

R1 yo k2tog k1 yo k2tog k17 k3 k2tog yo k2tog yo k2tog yo (k1 k2tog k3 k2tog k1 yo k1 yo k2tog yo k2tog yo) repeat ( ) one more time, k4 k17 k1 yo k2tog k2

R2 yo k2tog k1 yo k2tog p75 k1 yo k2tog k2

R3 yo k2tog k1 yo k2tog k7 k2tog yo yo k2tog k6 k3 k2tog yo k2tog yo k2tog yo (k1 k2tog k1 k2tog k1 yo k3 yo k2tog yo k2tog yo) repeat ( ) one more time, k4 k6 k2tog yo k2tog k7 k1 yo k2tog k2

R4 yo k2tog k1 yo k2tog p8, k1 p1 into loops, p7 p41 p7, k1 p1 into loops, p8 k1 yo k2tog k2

R5 yo k2tog k1 yo k2tog k17 k3 k2tog yo k2tog yo k2tog yo (k1, s11 k2tog psso, k1 yo k5 yo k2tog yo k2tog yo) repeat ( ) one more time, k4 k17 k1 yo k2tog k2

R6 yo k2tog k1 yo k2tog p75 k1 yo k2tog k2

R7 yo k2tog k1 yo k2tog k17 k4 yo k2tog yo k2tog (yo k1 yo k1 k2tog k3 k2tog k1 yo k2tog yo k2tog) repeat ( ) one more time, yo k2tog k3 k17 k1 yo k2tog k2

R8 yo k2tog k1 yo k2tog p75 k1 yo k2tog k2

R9 yo k2tog k1 yo k2tog k9 k2tog yo yo k2tog k4 k4 yo k2tog yo k2tog (yo k3 yo k1 k2tog k1 k2tog k1 yo k2tog yo k2tog) repeat ( ) one more time, yo k2tog k3 k4 k2tog yo yo k2tog k9 k1 yo k2tog k2

R10 yo k2tog k1 yo k2tog p10, k1 p1 into loops, p5 p41 p5, k1 p1 into loops, p10 k1 yo k2tog k2

R11 yo k2tog k1 yo k2tog k17 k4 yo k2tog yo k2tog (yo k5 yo k1, s11 k2tog psso, k1 yo k2tog yo k2tog) repeat ( ) one more time, yo k2tog k3 k17 k1 yo k2tog k2

R12 yo k2tog k1 yo k2tog p75 k1 yo k2tog k2

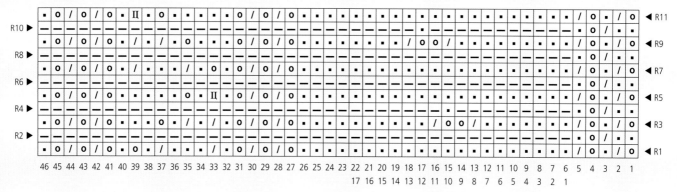

Chart showing the right-hand side of the back, with Lace Holes and Print of the Wave

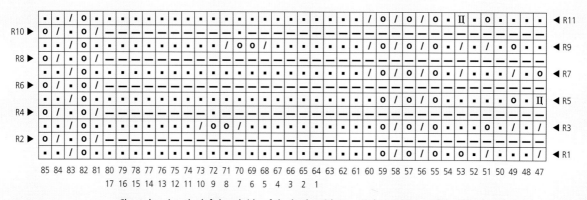

Chart showing the left-hand side of the back, with Lace Holes and Print of the Wave

Print of the wave without lace holes:

R13 yo k2tog k1 yo k2tog k17 k3 k2tog yo k2tog yo k2tog yo (k1 k2tog k3 k2tog k1 yo k1 yo k2tog yo k2tog yo) repeat ( ) one more time, k4 k17 k1 yo k2tog k2

R14 yo k2tog k1 yo k2tog p75 k1 yo k2tog k2

R15 yo k2tog k1 yo k2tog k17 k3 k2tog yo k2tog yo k2tog yo (k1 k2tog k1 k2tog k1 yo k3 yo k2tog yo k2tog yo) repeat ( ) one more time, k4 k17 k1 yo k2tog k2

R16 yo k2tog k1 yo k2tog p75 k1 yo k2tog k2

R17 yo k2tog k1 yo k2tog k17 k3 k2tog yo k2tog yo k2tog yo (k1, s11 k2tog psso, k1 yo k5 k2tog yo k2tog yo) repeat ( ) one more time, k4 k17 k1 yo k2tog k2

R18 yo k2tog k1 yo k2tog p75 k1 yo k2tog k2

R19 yo k2tog k1 yo k2tog k17 k4 yo k2tog yo k2tog (yo k1 yo k1 k2tog k3 k2tog k1 yo k2tog yo k2tog) repeat ( ) one more time, yo k2tog k3 k17 k1 yo k2tog k2

R20 yo k2tog k1 yo k2tog p75 k1 yo k2tog k2

R21 yo k2tog k1 yo k2tog k17 k4 yo k2tog yo k2tog (yo k3 yo k1 k2tog k1 k2tog k1 yo k2tog yo k2tog) repeat ( ) one more time, yo k2tog k3 k17 k1 yo k2tog k2

R22 yo k2tog k1 yo k2tog p75 k1 yo k2tog k2

R23 yo k2tog k1 yo k2tog k17 k4 yo k2tog yo k2tog (yo k5 yo k1, s11 k2tog psso, k1 yo k2tog yo k2tog) repeat ( ) one more time, yo k2tog k3 k17 k1 yo k2tog k2

R24 yo k2tog k1 yo k2tog p75 k1 yo k2tog k2

Repeat R1-R24 three more times

Repeat R1-12 one more time

BODICE (BACK)

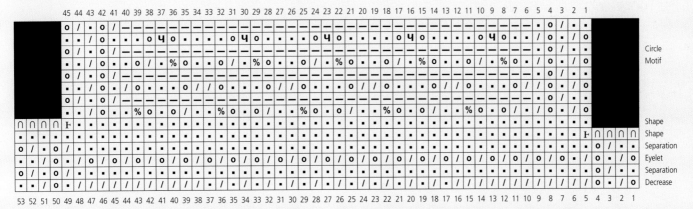

Chart showing the transition from the 85 sts of the main section into the 45 sts of Circle Motif of the Bodice

A decrease row is knitted. Switch to US 4 (3.5 mm) needles and knit a separation row. This is followed by an Eyelet row, another separation row, and two rows of shaping for the armholes. The first set of eight rows of Circle Motif are shown.

DECREASE
R1 yo k2tog k1 yo k2tog (k2tog) repeat ( ) ten more times, (k1 k2tog) repeat ( ) four more times, k1 (k2tog k1) repeat ( ) four more times, (k2tog) repeat ( ) ten more times, k1 yo k2tog k2

Switch to US 4 (3.5 mm) needles

Separation row:

R1 yo k2tog k1 yo k2tog k43 k1 yo k2tog k2 (53 sts)

EYELET

R1 yo k2tog k1 yo k2tog k1 (yo k2tog) repeat ( ) 20 more times, k1 yo k2tog k2

Separation row:

R1 yo k2tog k1yo k2tog k43 k1 yo k2tog k2

SHAPE FOR ARM HOLES

R1 bo 4 sts, k48

R2 bo 4 sts, k44

Front and back are the same up to this point

BODICE (BACK)

This section of 45 sts is worked continuing the 5-st loop and ladder at the beginning, 35 sts of circle motif and a 5-st ladder and loop at the end. Circle Motifs are multiples of 7 sts over 8 rows.

Circle motifs with loop and ladders:

R1 yo k2tog k1 yo k2tog (k1 k2tog yo k1 yo k2togb k1) repeat ( ) four more times, k1 yo k2tog k2

R2 yo k2tog k1 yo k2tog p35 k1 yo k2tog k2

R3 yo k2tog k1 yo k2tog (k2tog yo k3 yo k2tog) repeat ( ) four more times, k1 yo k2tog k2

R4 yo k2tog k1 yo k2tog p35 k1 yo k2tog k2

R5 yo k2tog k1 yo k2tog (k1 yo k2togb k1 k2tog yo k1) repeat ( ) four more times, k1 yo k2tog k2

R6 yo k2tog k1 yo k2tog p35 k1 yo k2tog k2

R7 yo k2tog k1 yo k2tog (k2 yo sskp yo k2) repeat ( ) four more times, k1 yo k2tog k2

R8 yo k2tog k1 yo k2tog p35 k1 yo k2tog k2

Repeat R1-R8 one more time

BACK OPENING

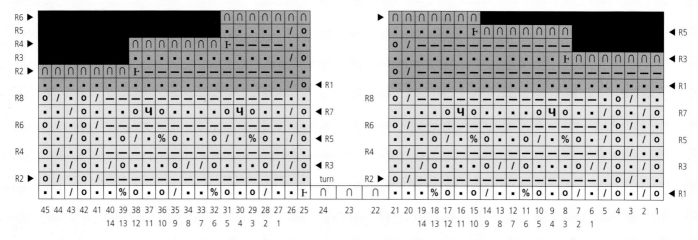

Chart showing the formation of the back opening within the Circle Motifs of the Bodice

(continued on page 62)

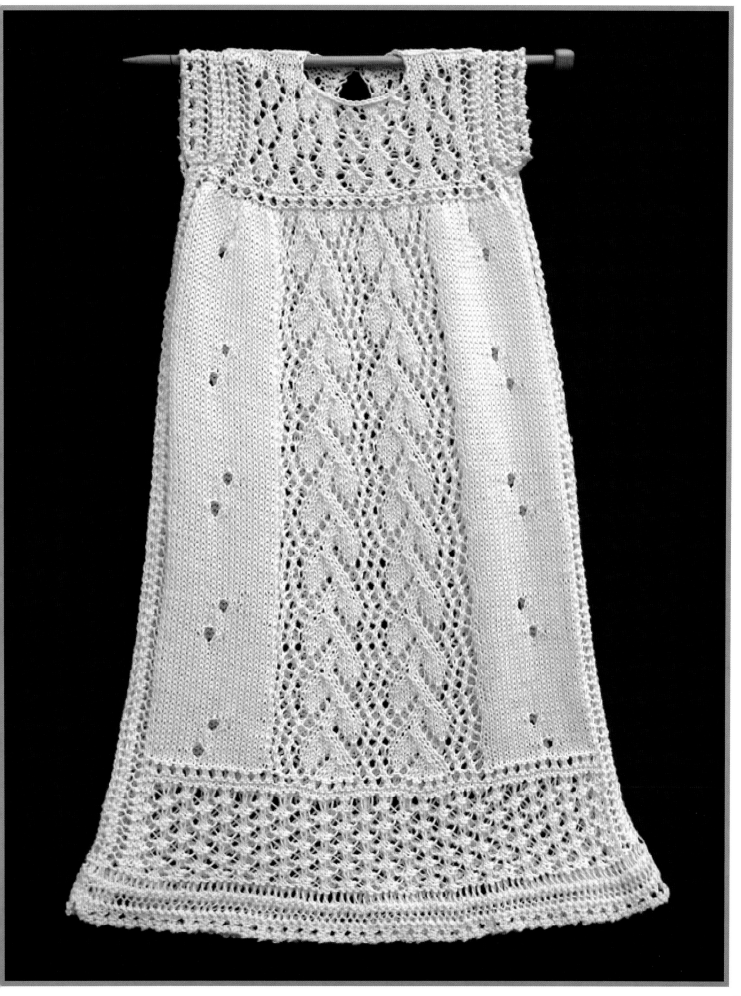

(continued from page 60)

Back opening row

R1 yo k2tog k1 yo k2tog (k1 k2tog yo k1 yo k2togb k1) repeat ( ) one more time, k2, bo 3 sts, k1 (k1 k2tog yo k1 yo k2togb k1) repeat ( ) one more time, k1 yo k2tog k2

Left side Circle motifs with loop and ladders

R2 yo k2tog k1 yo k2tog p14 k2, turn (leave remaining 21 sts on a spare needle)

R3 yo k2tog (k2tog yo k3 yo k2tog) repeat ( ) one more time, k1 yo k2tog k2

R4 yo k2tog k1 yo k2tog p14 k2

R5 yo k2tog (k1 yo k2togb k1 k2tog yo k1) repeat ( ) one more time, k1 yo k2tog k2

R6 yo k2tog k1 yo k2tog p14 k2

R7 yo k2tog (k2 yo sskp yo k2) repeat ( ) one more time, k1 yo k2tog k2

R8 yo k2tog k1 yo k2tog p14 k2

Shoulder shaping: left side of back

R1 yo k2tog k19

R2 bo 7 sts, p11 k2

R3 yo k2tog k12

R4 bo 7 sts, p4 k2

R5 yo k2tog k5

R6 bo all sts

Return to right side of back (R1 is already in place)

Re-join the yarn to the sts on the spare needle

R2 yo k2tog p14 k1 yo k2tog k2

R3 yo k2tog k1 yo k2tog (k2tog yo k3 yo k2tog) repeat ( ) one more time, k2

R4 yo k2tog p14 k1 yo k2tog k2

R5 yo k2tog k1 yo k2tog (k1 yo k2togb k1 k2tog yo k1) repeat ( ) one more time, k2

R6 yo k2tog p14 k1 yo k2tog k2

R7 yo k2tog k1 yo k2tog (k2 yo sskp yo k2) repeat ( ) one more time, k2

R8 yo k2tog p14 k1 yo k2tog k2

Shoulder shaping: right side of back

R1 k21

R2 yo k2tog p19

R3 bo 7 sts, k13

R4 yo k2tog p12

R5 bo 7 sts, k6

R6 bo all sts

FRONT

Repeat as for the Back up to the Bodice.

BODICE (FRONT)

This section of 45 sts is worked continuing the 5-st loop and ladder at the beginning, 35 sts of circle motif and a 5-st ladder and loop at the end.

Circle motifs with loop and ladders:

R1 yo k2tog k1 yo k2tog (k1 k2tog yo k1 yo k2togb k1) repeat ( ) four more times, k1 yo k2tog k2

R2 yo k2tog k1 yo k2tog p35 k1 yo k2tog k2

R3 yo k2tog k1 yo k2tog (k2tog yo k3 yo k2tog) repeat ( ) four more times, k1 yo k2tog k2

R4 yo k2tog k1 yo k2tog p35 k1 yo k2tog k2

R5 yo k2tog k1 yo k2tog (k1 yo k2togb k1 k2tog yo k1) repeat ( ) four more times, k1 yo k2tog k2

R6 yo k2tog k1 yo k2tog p35 k1 yo k2tog k2

R7 yo k2tog k1 yo k2tog (k2 yo sskp yo k2) repeat ( ) four more times, k1 yo k2tog k2

R8 yo k2tog k1 yo k2tog p35 k1 yo k2tog k2

Repeat R1-R8 two more times

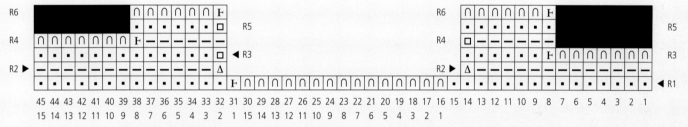

Chart showing the formation of the neck and shoulder shaping above the Circle Motif of the Bodice

---

NECK AND SHOULDER SHAPING

R1 k15, bo 15sts, k14

R2 p13 p2tog, turn, leave remaining 15 sts on a spare needle

R3 slk, k13

R4 bo 7 sts, p6

R5 slk, k6

R6 bo all sts

Re-join the yarn to the sts on the spare needle

R2 p2tog p13

R3 bo 7 sts, k6

R4 slk, p6

R6 k7

R7 bo all sts

BODICE CUFFS (USING US 4 NEEDLES)
Co 8 sts firmly
Knit one row

Pattern:
R1 yo k2tog k1 yo k2tog k1 yo yo k2
R2 slk k1 k1 p1 k1 k1 yo k2tog k2
R3 yo k2tog k1 yo k2tog k3 k2tog
R4 bo 1 st, k2 k1 yo k2tog k2

Repeat R1-R4 11 more times

Yo k2tog, k to end of row
Bo all sts firmly

Repeat this for the second cuff and attach cuffs to bodice.

BLOCKING
Back, front and cuffs are now blocked.

Blocking requires some time, but is essential for the final appearance of the shawl. Putting the robe pieces in water releases the tension in the stitches.

The method I use is:

1. Remove the stitch markers and briefly put the knitted pieces in a container, into the temperature of water indicated on the label for washing instructions, ensuring pieces are entirely submerged

2. Drain the water from the container

3. Very gently, squeeze any excess water from the pieces

4. Wrap the pieces in a large clean towel to absorb moisture; when the towel is damp, change to a new towel and repeat until only slightly damp

5. Remove the pieces from the towel and place on a large sheet on the floor

6. In a room where the pieces can air dry as long as needed with the door closed to keep pets away from your work, spread the pieces out to form a good shape

7. All the loops that have been worked have a pin placed in them

8. Also place pins in each circle of the edging

Note I do not recommend use of a spray bottle in place of the immersion process described above.

When dry, trace around the back and front to make a pattern for a fabric underskirt if required.

Newborn Baby Shoes

MATERIALS
• Small amount 1-ply Shetland lace wool (also known as single), small amount of coloured yarn or thread for decoration, needle to sew seams

NEEDLES
• Two US 1 (2.5 mm) needles and one US 2 (2.75 mm) needle for bo

SIZE
• 3" long x 1" deep

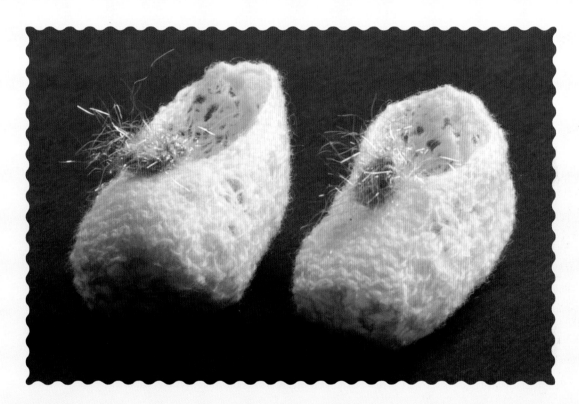

Instructions

Cast on 34 stitches firmly

Knit one row

R1 k1 yo k15 yo k1 yo k1 yo k15 yo k1

R2 and alternate rows up to and including row 12: k, with the yo's from the previous row being worked as kb

R3 k2 yo k15 yo k3 yo k2 yo k15 yo k2

R5 k3 yo k15 yo k4 yo k4 yo k15 yo k3

R7 k4 yo k15 yo k6 yo k5 yo k15 yo k4

R9 k5 yo k15 yo k7 yo k7 yo k15 yo k5

R11 k21 yo k9 yo k8 yo k21 (62 sts)

R12: k, with the yo's from the previous row being worked as kb

WORK 9 ROWS IN RING STITCH

R1 k1 k2 yo k3tog (yo k3 yo k3tog) repeat ( ) eight more times, yo k2

R2 k1 (k2tog yo k1 yo k2tog k1) repeat ( ) nine more times, k1

R3 k2 k2tog (yo k1 yo k2tog yo k3tog) repeat ( ) eight more times, yo k1 yo k2tog k1

R4 k1 (k2tog yo k1 yo k2tog k1) repeat ( ) nine more times, k1

R5 k1 k2tog yo k3 yo (k3tog yo k3 yo) repeat ( ) eight more times, k2tog

R6 k1 (yo k2tog k1 k2tog yo k1) repeat ( ) nine more times, k1

R7 k1 (k1 yo k2tog yo k3tog yo) repeat ( ) nine more times, k1
R8 k1 (yo k2tog k1 k2tog yo k1) repeat ( ) nine more times, k1
R9 repeat row 1

Knit 2 rows in garter stitch

SHAPE INSTEP
next row: k35 k2tog turn, leaving 25 sts on the left hand needle
next row: slk k8 k2tog turn
repeat this row 16 more times

next row: slk k26
next row: k16 k2tog k8 k2tog k16
next row: k

Bo all sts using the larger needle

Join sole and heel seam
Knit second shoe
Block shoes and add decoration if required

Premature Baby Shoes

MATERIALS
• Small amount of No 30 Cotton Thread, small amount of coloured yarn or thread for decoration, needle to sew seams

NEEDLES
• Two US 0 (2 mm) needles and one US 1 (2.50 mm) needle for bo, needle to sew seams

SIZE
• 2¾" long x ¾" deep

Instructions

Cast on 34 stitches firmly

R1 k1 yo k15 yo k1 yo k1 yo k15 yo k1

R2 and alternate rows up to and including row 10: k, with the yo's from the previous row being worked as kb

R3 k2 yo k15 yo k3 yo k2 yo k15 yo k2

R5 k3 yo k15 yo k4 yo k4 yo k15 yo k3

R7 k4 yo k15 yo k6 yo k5 yo k15 yo k4

R9 k5 yo k15 yo k7 yo k7 yo k15 yo k5

R11 k21 yo k9 yo k8 yo k21 (62 sts)

R12: k, with the yo's from the previous row being worked as kb

---

WORK 9 ROWS IN BEAD STITCH

R1 k3 (yo k3tog yo k3) repeat ( ) eight more times, yo k3tog yo k2

R2 k1 (k2tog yo k1 yo k2tog k1) repeat ( ) nine more times, k1

R3 k1 k2tog (yo k3 yo k3tog) repeat ( ) eight more times, yo k3 yo k2tog

R4 k1 (yo k2tog k1 k2tog yo k1) repeat ( ) nine more times, k1

R5-8 Repeat rows 1-4 one more time

R9 Repeat row 1

Knit 2 rows

SHAPE INSTEP

Next row: k35 k2tog turn, leaving 25 sts on the left hand needle

Next row: slk k8 k2tog turn

Repeat this row 16 more times

Next row: slk k26

Next row: k16 k2tog k8 k2tog k16

Knit one row

Bo all sts using larger needle

Join sole and heel seam

Knit second shoe

Block shoes and add decoration if required

WEARABLE LACE

The yarn industry has moved in leaps and bounds in the last several years and wearable lace knitting has been part of the movement. Lace can be worked in all kinds of yarn with the right pattern stitches. The pieces represent today's new lace knitting world where anything is possible.

Lace Ladder Scarf

MATERIALS
• 2 balls Patons Bohemian yarn, Wandering Wines. 80g ball (62 m/ 68 yd)

NEEDLES
• US 17 (12 mm) needles

SIZE
• 68" (not including fringe) x 6"

Instructions

This pattern is a simple lace ladder. After casting on, knot the end of the yarn to prevent possible unravelling. Remove the knot to sew up. The slk on each row forms a firm edge. One ball makes a scarf 52" long with no fringe.

Co 12 st loosely
Knit 1 row

R1: slk yo k2tog (k1 yo k2tog) repeat ( ) two more times

Repeat to desired length
Knit 1 row
Bo all st loosely

Add fringe if desired, splitting the yarn for a different effect.

R2 ▶	□	o	/	·	o	/	·	o	/	·	o	/	
	/	o	·	/	o	·	/	o	·	/	o	□	◀ R1
	12	11	10	9	8	7	6	5	4	3	2	1	

Cable Hat

MATERIALS
• 1 ball Patons Shetland Chunky, Lilac Lace. 100 g (136 m/148 yds) ball

NEEDLES
• US 8 (5 mm) and US 10 (6 mm) needles, one size 10 cable needle, needle to sew seam and weave in ends

SIZE
• 20½" circumference, 8¼" deep

Instructions

The 3 cable rows can be a little tricky, but it is worth the effort. The lace cable and reverse stocking stitch pattern has rows 7, 19 and 31 as the cable cross over rows. The cables continue into the decreases for six rows.

Using the size 8 needles, cast on 80 sts firmly
Work 4 rows in stocking stitch (the rollup)
Change to the size 10 needles

CABLE PATTERN (SEE PATTERN PAGE 72)
R1 p2 (*k2tog yo k2* repeat * to * 2 more times, p4) repeat ( ) three more times, *k2tog yo k2* repeat * to * 2 more times, p2

R2 k2 (*p2tog yrn p2* repeat * to * 2 more times, k4) repeat ( ) three more times, *p2tog yrn p2* repeat * to * 2 more times, k2

R3, 4 repeat R1, R2

R5, 6 repeat R1, R2

R7 p2 (*k2tog yo k1, slip the next 3 sts onto cable needle and hold at back of work, k1 k2tog from left hand needle needle, yo, k2 from the cable needle, knit next st on left hand needle and last st on cable needle together, yo k2* p4) repeat ( ) three more times, repeat * to * one more time, p2

R8 repeat R2

R9-18 repeat R1, R2 five times

R19 repeat R7

R20 repeat R2

R21-30 repeat R1, R2 five times

R31 repeat R7

R32 repeat R2

R33-34 repeat R1, R2

DECREASE ROWS
R1 p2tog (*k2tog yo k2 k2tog k2tog k2tog yo k2* p2tog p2tog) repeat ( ) three more times, repeat * to * one more time, p2tog (60 sts)

R2 k1 (*p2tog yrn p2 p2 p2tog yrn p2* k2) repeat ( ) three more times, repeat * to * one more time, k1 (60 sts)

R3 p1 (k2tog five times, p2tog) repeat ( ) three more times, k2tog five times, p1 (31 sts)

R4 k1 (p5 k1) repeat ( ) four more times (31 sts)

R5 k2tog to last st, k1 (16 sts)

R6 p2tog to end of row (8 sts)

Thread yarn through the 8 sts, sew seam on the inside from crown to beginning of cables, then on the outside for the 4 stocking st rows.

80	79	78	77	76	75	74	73	72	71	70	69	68	67
·	·	Δ	◇	—	—	Δ	◇	—	—	Δ	◇	—	—
—	—	·	·	o	/	·	·	o	/	·	·	o	/
·	·	Δ	◇	—	—	Δ	◇	—	—	Δ	◇	—	—
—	—	·	·	o	/	·	·	o	/	·	·	o	/
·	·	Δ	◇	—	—	Δ	◇	—	—	Δ	◇	—	—
—	—	cable section										
·	·	Δ	◇	—	—	Δ	◇	—	—	Δ	◇	—	—
—	—	·	·	o	/	·	·	o	/	·	·	o	/
·	·	Δ	◇	—	—	Δ	◇	—	—	Δ	◇	—	—
—	—	·	·	o	/	·	·	o	/	·	·	o	/
R2 ▶ ·	·	Δ	◇	—	—	Δ	◇	—	—	Δ	◇	—	—
—	—	·	·	o	/	·	·	o	/	·	·	o	/

repeat over 64 sts (middle cable section chart)

2	1
·	·
—	—
·	·
—	—
·	·
—	— **R7**
·	·
—	—
·	·
—	—
·	·
—	— **◀ R1**

Chart of main pattern of the hat showing cable and separator stitches. Refer to text R7 for cable row

Fingerless Lace Gloves

MATERIALS
• 1ball Patons Stretch Socks Yarn, Black Taffy. 50g ball (219 m/ 239 yd)

NEEDLES
• Four double pointed US 2 (2.75 mm) needles, stitch markers

SIZE
• To fit average hand

Instructions

KNITTED IN ROUNDS (RD)
Co 56 sts

Divide onto three needles: needle 1:16; needle 2:20; needle 3:20

Rd1-Rd22 k1 p1 rib

Rd23 [needle 1] k1, place marker on this first st, k6, k1, place marker on this st (8 sts for thumb gusset) k8 (16 sts)

[needle 2] k (20 sts)

[needle 3] k (20 sts)

THUMB GUSSET INCREASE AND PATTERN PLACEMENT
Rd1 [needle 1] k1, k1 into front and back of next st, (k2tog yo yo k2tog), k1 into front and back of next st, k1, (k2tog yo yo k2tog) repeat ( ) one more time (18 sts)

[needle 2] (k2tog yo yo k2tog) repeat ( ) four more times (20 sts)

[needle 3] (k2tog yo yo k2tog) repeat ( ) four more times (20 sts)

Rd2 [needle 1] k3 (k1, k1 p1 into yos, k1) k3 (k1, k1 p1 into yos, k1) repeat ( ) one more time

[needle 2] (k1, k1 p1 into yos, k1) repeat ( ) four more times

[needle 3] (k1, k1 p1 into yos, k1) repeat ( ) four more times

Rd3 [all needles] k

Continue with thumb gusset increases on Rd1 working the increase sts as k sts until 24 sts are between the markers. Work Rd2 one more time.

[needle 1] k 24 sts, slip them onto a piece of yarn and secure

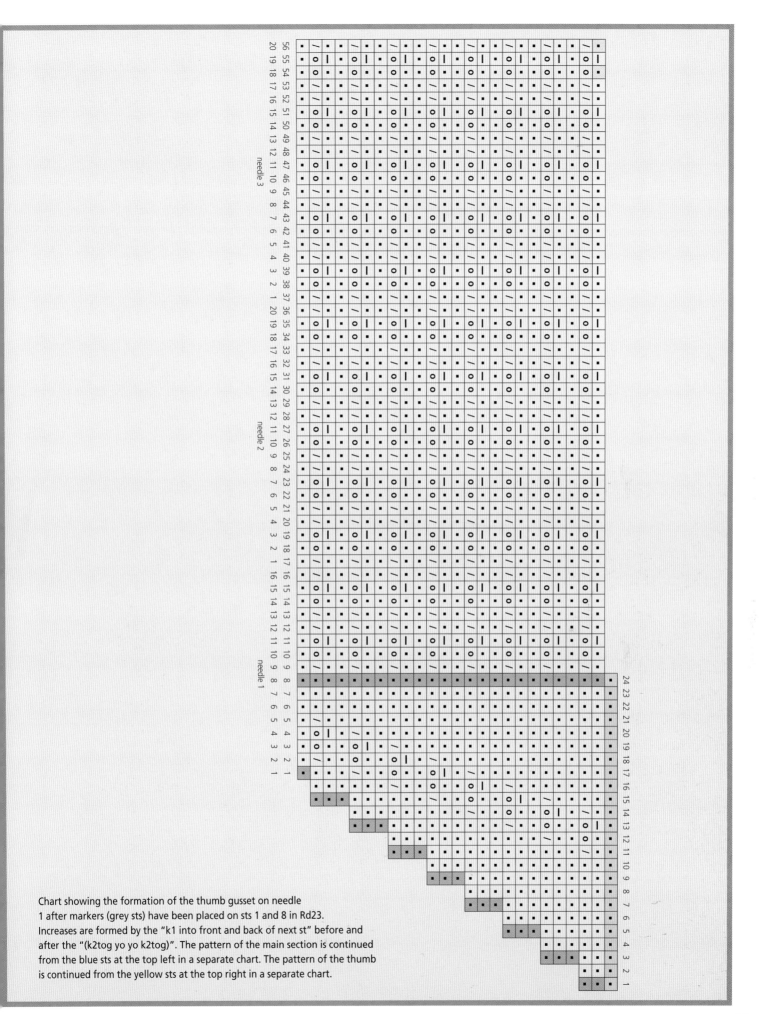

Chart showing the formation of the thumb gusset on needle
1 after markers (grey sts) have been placed on sts 1 and 8 in Rd23.
Increases are formed by the "k1 into front and back of next st" before and
after the "(k2tog yo yo k2tog)". The pattern of the main section is continued
from the blue sts at the top left in a separate chart. The pattern of the thumb
is continued from the yellow sts at the top right in a separate chart.

Returning to the first needle, co 8 sts *
Work Rd3 on all three needles
Needle 1:16 sts, needle 2:20, needle 3:20

Rd1 [needle 1] (k2tog yo yo k2tog) repeat ( ) three more times (16 sts)
[needle 2] (k2tog yo yo k2tog) repeat ( ) four more times (20 sts)
[needle 3] (k2tog yo yo k2tog) repeat ( ) four more times (20 sts)
Rd2 [needle 1] (k1, k1 p1 into yos, k1) repeat ( ) three more times
[needle 2] (k1, k1 p1 into yos, k1) repeat ( ) four more times
[needle 3] (k1, k1 p1 into yos, k1) repeat ( ) four more times
Rd3 [all needles] k

Continue with this pattern four more times

Change to k1 p1 rib for two rounds

Bo all sts

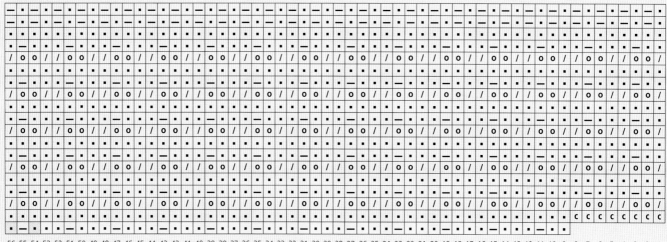

Chart showing the continuation of the main section with 8 co sts following the separation of the thumb

RETURN TO THUMB GUSSET
Return the 24 sts back to a needle, divide sts as follows

With the inside of the thumb gusset facing you:

Rd1 [needle 1]: pick up 6 sts along the 8 st cast on (see * earlier in the pattern), k4 from the needle with the 24 sts
[needle 2]: k6 k2tog yo yo k2tog k2
[needle 3]: k8
Rd2 [needle 1] k10

[needle 2] k6 k1, k1 p1 into yos, k1 k2
[needle 3] k8
Rd3 [all needles] k

Knit k1 p1 rib for two rounds
Bo all sts

30	29	28	27	26	25	24	23	22	21	20	19	18	17	16	15	14	13	12	11	10	9	8	7	6	5	4	3	2	1
—	•	—	•	—	•	—	•	—	•	—	•	—	•	—	•	—	•	—	•	—	•	—	•	—	•	—	•	—	•
—	•	—	•	—	•	—	•	—	•	—	•	—	•	—	•	—	•	—	•	—	•	—	•	—	•	—	•	—	•
•	•	•	•	•	•	•	•	•	•	•	•	•	•	•	•	•	•	•	•	•	•	•	•	•	•	•	•	•	•
•	•	•	•	•	•	•	•	•	•	•	—	•	•	•	•	•	•	•	•	•	•	•	•	•	•	•	•	•	•
•	•	•	•	•	•	•	•	•	•	/	o	o	/	•	•	•	•	•	•	•	•	•	•	x	x	x	x	x	x
•	•	•	•	•	•	•	•	•	•	•	•	•	•	•	•	•	•	•	•	•	•	•	•	c	c	c	c	c	c

| 8 | 7 | 6 | 5 | 4 | 3 | 2 | 1 | 12 | 11 | 10 | 9 | 8 | 7 | 6 | 5 | 4 | 3 | 2 | 1 | 10 | 9 | 8 | 7 | 6 | 5 | 4 | 3 | 2 | 1 |

needle 3   needle 2   needle 1

Chart showing completion of the thumb. x: st picked up from 6 of the the 8 st cast on.
The yellow stitches are those indicated in the earlier chart.

Leg Warmers

MATERIALS
• 1 ball Lion Brand Sock-Ease Yarn, Circus Peanut. 100g (438 yd/400 m) ball

NEEDLES
• US 2 (2.75 mm), large-eyed blunt needle for weaving in ends

SIZE
• 11" circumference at knee, 7" at ankle; 13" long

Instructions

Co 96 sts on one needle

Divide sts onto 3 needles as follows, k1 p1 rib as you divide:
Needle 1: 28 sts, needle 2: 40 sts, needle 3: 28 sts

Work 26 rounds of k1 p1 rib

Pattern begins (Honeycomb reverse stocking stitch pattern)
Rd1 needle 1: p4 (k2tog yo yo k2tog) repeat ( ) three more times, p8
        needle 2: (k2tog yo yo k2tog) repeat ( ) three more times, p8 (k2tog yo yo k2tog) repeat ( ) three more times
        needle 3: p8 (k2tog yo yo k2tog) repeat ( ) three more times, p4
Rd2 needle 1: p4 (k1, k1 p1 into yos, k1) repeat ( ) three more times, p8
        needle 2: (k1, k1 p1 into yos, k1) repeat ( ) three more times, p8 (k1, k1 p1 into yos, k1) repeat ( ) three more times
        needle 3: p8 (k1, k1 p1 into yos, k1) repeat ( ) three more times, p4
Rd3 needle 1: p4 k2 (k2tog yo yo k2tog) repeat ( ) two more times, k2 p8
        needle 2: k2 (k2tog yo yo k2tog) repeat ( ) two more times, k2 p8 k2 (k2tog yo yo k2tog) repeat ( ) two more times, k2
        needle 3: p8 k2 (k2tog yo yo k2tog) repeat ( ) two more times, k2 p4
Rd4 needle 1: p4 k2 (k1, k1 p1 into yos, k1) repeat ( ) two more times, k2 p8
        needle 2: k2 (k1, k1 p1 into yos, k1) repeat ( ) two more times, k2 p8 k2 (k1, k1 p1 into yos, k1) repeat ( ) two more times, k2
        needle 3: p8 k2 (k1, k1 p1 into yos, k1) repeat ( ) two more times, k2 p4

Chart of the 96 sts of the four pattern rounds. The shaded stitches indicate the first and last stitch on needle 2.

Repeat Rd1-Rd4 21 more times

Repeat Rd1-Rd2 one more time

Decrease rounds

Rd1 needle 1: p1 p2tog p1 k2 (k2tog yo yo k2tog) repeat ( ) two more times, k2 p1 p2tog p2 p2tog p1 (25 sts)

needle 2: k2 (k2tog yo yo k2tog) repeat ( ) two more times, k2 p1 p2tog p2 p2tog p1 k2 (k2tog yo yo k2tog) repeat ( ) two more times, k2 (38 sts)

needle 3: p1 p2tog p2 p2tog p1 k2 (k2tog yo yo k2tog) repeat ( ) two more times, k2 p1 p2tog p1 (25 sts)

Rd2 needle 1: p1 p2tog k2 (k1, k1 p1 into yos, k1) repeat ( ) two more times, k2 p1 p2tog p2tog p1 (22 sts)

needle 2: k2 (k1, k1 p1 into yos, k1) repeat ( ) two more times, k2 p1 p2tog p2tog p1 k2 (k1, k1 p1 into yos, k1) repeat ( ) two more times, k2 (36 sts)

needle 3: p1 p2tog p2tog p1 k2 (k1, k1 p1 into yos, k1) repeat ( ) two more times, k2 p1 p2tog (22 sts)

Ankle rib (80 sts)

K1 p1 rib for 18 rounds

Bo all sts

LACE WRAPS

1. Lace Wrap 1
2. Lace Wrap 2 (page 90)

Wraps can be be worked in various lengths and widths. All have the same purpose: to embrace or enhance the body while providing warmth and cover. Wraps where the back and the front are worked in different detail provide a soft mirroring in the front pieces and a dramatic effect on the back. Wraps can be worn from either side.

Lace Wrap 1

MATERIALS
• 8 balls Patons Angora Bamboo Yarn, Urban Grey. 50g ball (73 m/ 80 yds)

NEEDLES
• US 10 (6 mm), needle for weaving in ends

SIZE
• 16" x 56"

Instructions

There are 75 sts on this wrap, 71 sts for the Shetland Twin and two Seed Stitches on either side. The left and right hand side of the front are done in the Shetland Twin. Other pattern sts include Lace Holes, Eyelids and Medallion.

Co 75 sts
Knit one row

RIGHT FRONT SECTION

Shetland Twin 14 sts +1, over 18 rows. The +1 is a k1 at the beginning of the odd rows and a p1 at the end of the even rows.

5-SHETLAND TWIN SECTION
R1 k1 p1 k1 (k4 k2tog yo k1 yo skp k5) repeat ( ) four more times, p1 k1
R2 k1 p1 (p4 p2togb yrn p3 yrn p2tog p3) repeat ( ) four more times, p1 p1 k1
R3 k1 p1 k1 (k2 k2tog yo k2tog yo k1 yo skp yo skp k3) repeat ( ) four more times, p1 k1
R4 k1 p1 (p2 p2togb yrn p2togb yrn p3 yrn p2tog yrn p2tog p1) repeat ( ) four more times, p1 p1 k1
R5 k1 p1 k1 (k2tog yo k2 yo skp k1 k2tog yo k2 yo skp k1) repeat ( ) four more times, p1 k1
R6 k1 p1 (p1 yrn p2tog p3 yrn p3tog yrn p3 p2togb yrn) repeat ( ) four more times, p1 p1 k1
R7 k1 p1 k1 (yo skp k2 k2tog yo k1 yo skp k2 k2tog yo k1) repeat ( ) four more times, p1 k1

R8 k1 p1 (p1 yrn p2tog p1 p2togb yrn p3 yrn p2tog p1 p2togb yrn) repeat ( ) four more times, p1 p1 k1

R9 k1 p1 k1 (yo skp k2 yo skp k1 k2tog yo k2 k2tog yo k1) repeat ( ) four more times, p1 k1

R10 repeat R6

R11 repeat R7

R12 repeat R8

R13 k1 p1 k1 (k1 yo skp k1 yo skp k1 k2tog yo k1 k2tog yo k2) repeat ( ) four more times, p1 k1

R14 k1 p1 (p3 yrn p2tog p1 yrn p3tog yrn p1 p2togb yrn p2) repeat ( ) four more times, p1 p1 k1

R15 k1 p1 k1 (k3 yo skp k3 k2tog yo k4) repeat ( ) four more times, p1 k1

R16 k1 p1 (p5 yrn p2tog p1 p2togb yrn p4) repeat ( ) four more times, p1 p1 k1

R17 k1 p1 k1 (k5 yo, sl1 k2tog psso, yo k6) repeat ( ) four more times, p1 k1

R18 k1 p73 k1

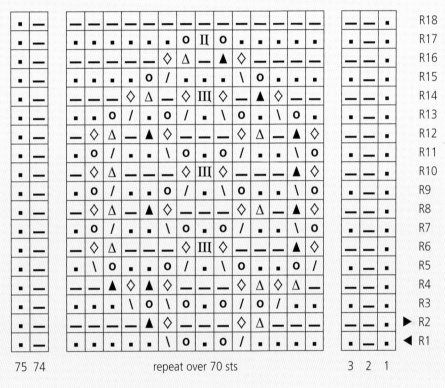

Chart of the 5-Shetland Twin section

Repeat R1-R18 two more times

3-SHETLAND TWIN SECTION WITH EYELID ON EACH SIDE (R55-R72)
Eyelid stitches are also in ( ) although no repeat

R1 k1 p1 k15 (k4 k2tog yo k1 yo skp k5) repeat ( ) two more times, k14 p1 k1

R2 k1 p1 p14 (p4 p2togb yrn p3 yrn p2tog p3) repeat ( ) two more times, p15 p1 k1

R3 k1 p1 k15 (k2 k2tog yo k2tog yo k1 yo skp yo skp k3) repeat ( ) two more times, k14 p1 k1

R4 k1 p1 p14 (p2 p2togb yrn p2togb yrn p3 yrn p2tog yrn p2tog p1) repeat ( ) two more times, p15 p1 k1

R5 k1 p1 k15 (k2tog yo k2 yo skp k1 k2tog yo k2 yo skp k1) repeat ( ) two more times, k14 p1 k1

R6 k1 p1 p14 (p1 yrn p2tog p3 yrn p3tog yrn p3 p2togb yrn) repeat ( ) two more times, p15 p1 k1

R7 k1 p1 k4 (k1 k2tog yo k1 yo k2tog k1) k4 (yo skp k2 k2tog yo k1 yo skp k2 k2tog yo k1) repeat ( ) two more times, k3 (k1 k2tog yo k1 yo k2tog k1) k4 p1 k1

R8 k1 p1 p4 (p2tog yrn p3 yrn p2tog) p3 (p1 yrn p2tog p1 p2togb yrn p3 yrn p2tog p1 p2togb yrn) repeat ( ) two more times, p4 (p2tog yrn p3 yrn p2tog) p4 p1 k1

R9 k1 p1 k4 (k7) k4 (yo skp k2 yo skp k1 k2tog yo k2 k2tog yo k1) repeat ( ) two more times, k3 (k7) k4 p1 k1

R10 k1 p1 p4 (p1 yrn p2tog yrn p3tog yrn p1) p3 (p1 yrn p2tog p3 yrn p3tog yrn p3 p2togb yrn) repeat ( ) two more times, p4 (p1 yrn p2tog yrn p3tog yrn p1) p4 p1 k1

R11 k1 p1 k4 (k7) k4 (yo skp k2 k2tog yo k1 yo skp k2 k2tog yo k1) repeat ( ) two more times, k3 (k7) k4 p1 k1

R12 k1 p1 p4 (p2 yrn p3tog yrn p2) p3 (p1 yrn p2tog p1 p2togb yrn p3 yrn p2tog p1 p2togb yrn) repeat ( ) two more times, p4 (p2 yrn p3tog yrn p2) p4 p1 k1

R13 k1 p1 k15 (k1 yo skp k1 yo skp k1 k2tog yo k1 k2tog yo k2) repeat ( ) two more times, k14 p1 k1

R14 k1 p1 p14 (p3 yrn p2tog p1 yrn p3tog yrn p1 p2togb yrn p2) repeat ( ) two more times, p15 p1 k1

R15 k1 p1 k15 (k3 yo skp k3 k2tog yo k4) repeat ( ) two more times, k14 p1 k1

R16 k1 p1 p14 (p5 yrn p2tog p1 p2togb yrn p4) repeat ( ) two more times, p15 p1 k1

R17 k1 p1 k15 (k5 yo, sl1 k2tog psso, yo k6) repeat ( ) two more times, k14 p1 k1

R18 k1 p73 k1

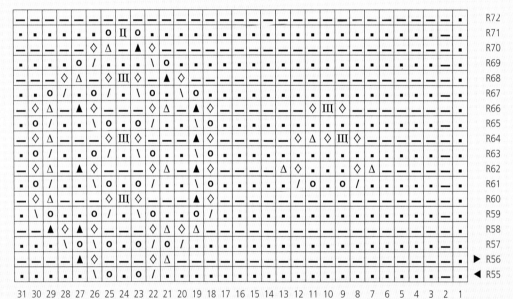

Chart showing 1 Shetland Twin and the Eyelid at the right hand side of the 3-Shetland Twin section.

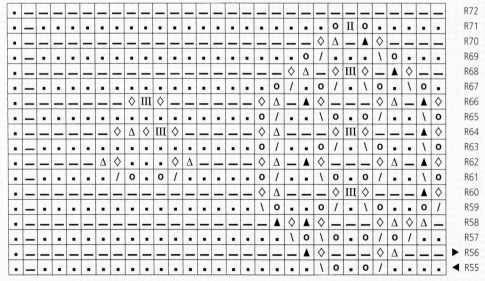

Chart showing left hand Shetland Twin and Eyelid in the 3-Twin section

1-SHETLAND TWIN SECTION WITH EYELID ON EACH SIDE (R73-R90)

R1 k1 p1 k29 (k4 k2tog yo k1 yo skp k5) k28 p1 k1

R2 k1 p1 p28 (p4 p2togb yrn p3 yrn p2tog p3) p29 p1 k1

R3 k1 p1 k29 (k2 k2tog yo k2tog yo k1 yo skp yo skp k3) k28 p1 k1

R4 k1 p1 p28 (p2 p2togb yrn p2togb yrn p3 yrn p2tog yrn p2tog p1) p29 p1 k1

R5 k1 p1 k29 (k2tog yo k2 yo skp k1 k2tog yo k2 yo skp k1) k28 p1 k1

R6 k1 p1 p28 (p1 yrn p2tog p3 yrn p3tog yrn p3 p2togb yrn) p29 p1 k1

R7 k1 p1 k18 (k1 k2tog yo k1 yo k2tog k1) k4 (yo skp k2 k2tog yo k1 yo skp k2 k2tog yo k1) k3 (k1 k2tog yo k1 yo k2tog k1) k18 p1 k1

R8 k1 p1 p18 (p2tog yrn p3 yrn p2tog) p3 (p1 yrn p2tog p1 p2togb yrn p3 yrn p2tog p1 p2togb yrn) p4 (p2tog yrn p3 yrn p2tog) p18 p1 k1

R9 k1 p1 k18 (k7) k4 (yo skp k2 yo skp k1 k2tog yo k2 k2tog yo k1) k3 (k7) k18 p1 k1

R10 k1 p1 p18 (p1 yrn p2tog yrn p3tog yrn p1) p3 (p1 yrn p2tog p3 yrn p3tog yrn p3 p2togb yrn) p4 (p1 yrn p2tog yrn p3tog yrn p1) p18 p1 k1

R11 k1 p1 k18 (k7) k4 (yo skp k2 k2tog yo k1 yo skp k2 k2tog yo k1) k3 (k7) k18 p1 k1

R12 k1 p1 p18 (p2 yrn p3tog yrn p2) p3 (p1 yrn p2tog p1 p2togb yrn p3 yrn p2tog p1 p2togb yrn) p4 (p2 yrn p3tog yrn p2) p18 p1 k1

R13 k1 p1 k29 (k1 yo skp k1 yo skp k1 k2tog yo k1 k2tog yo k2) k28 p1 k1

R14 k1 p1 p28 (p3 yrn p2tog p1 yrn p3tog yrn p1 p2togb yrn p2) p29 p1 k1

R15 k1 p1 k29 (k3 yo skp k3 k2tog yo k4) k28 p1 k1

R16 k1 p1 p28 (p5 yrn p2tog p1 p2togb yrn p4) p29 p1 k1

R17 k1 p1 k29 (k5 yo, sl1 k2tog psso, yo k6) k28 p1 k1

R18 k1 p73 k1

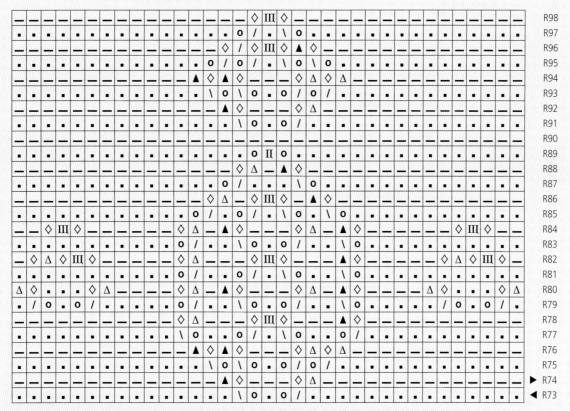

Chart showing 1-Shetland Twin and Eyelid and the Medallion above it.

MEDALLION (R91-R98)

R1 k1 p1 k30 k3 k2tog yo k1 yo sl1k1psso k3 k30 p1 k1

R2 k1 p1 p30 p2 p2togb yrn p3 yrn p2tog p2 p30 p1 k1

R3 k1 p1 k30 k1 k2tog yo k2tog yo k1 yo skp yo skp k1 k30 p1 k1

R4 k1 p1 p30 p2togb yrn p2togb yrn p3 yrn p2tog yrn p2tog p30 p1 k1

R5 k1 p1 k30 k1 yo skp yo skp k1 k2tog yo k2tog yo k1 k30 p1 k1

R6 k1 p1 p30 p2 yrn p2tog yrn p3tog yrn p2togb yrn p2 p30 p1 k1

R7 k1 p1 k30 k3 yo skp k1 k2tog yo k3 k30 p1 k1

R8 k1 p1 p30 p4 yrn p3tog yrn p4 p30 p1 k1

SEPARATION ROWS

R99 k1 p1 k71 p1 k1

R100 k1 p1 p71 p1 k1

MIDDLE SECTION

EYELIDS AND LACE HOLES

R1 k1 p1 k31 (k2tog yo yo k2tog) k1 (k2tog yo yo k2tog) k31 p1 k1

R2 k1 p1 p31 (p1 k1 p1 p1) p1 (p1 k1 p1 p1) p31 p1 k1

R3 k1 p1 k29 (k2tog yo yo k2tog) k5 (k2tog yo yo k2tog) k29 p1 k1

R4 k1 p1 p29 (p1 k1 p1 p1) p5 (p1 k1 p1 p1) p29 p1 k1

R5 k1 p1 k27 (k2tog yo yo k2tog) k1 (k1 k2tog yo k1 yo k2tog k1) k1 (k2tog yo yo k2tog) k27 p1 k1

R6 k1 p1 p27 (p1 k1 p1 p1) p1 (p2tog yrn p3 yrn p2tog) p1 (p1 k1 p1 p1) p27 p1 k1

R7 k1 p1 k25 (k2tog yo yo k2tog) k3 (k7) k3 (k2tog yo yo k2tog) k25 p1 k1

R8 k1 p1 p25 (p1 k1 p1 p1) p3 (p1 yrn p2tog yrn p3tog yrn p1) p3 (p1 k1 p1 p1) p25 p1 k1

R9 k1 p1 k23 (k2tog yo yo k2tog) k5 (k7) k5 (k2tog yo yo k2tog) k23 p1 k1

R10 k1 p1 p23 (p1 k1 p1 p1) p5 (p2 yrn p3tog yrn p2) p5 (p1 k1 p1 p1) p23 p1 k1

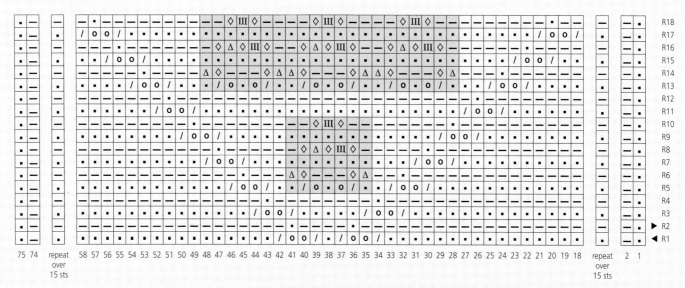

Chart showing the start of the middle section, with 1 and 3 Eyelids bordered by Lace Holes.

(continued on page 88)

(continued from page 86)

R11 k1 p1 k21 (k2tog yo yo k2tog) k21 (k2tog yo yo k2tog) k21 p1 k1

R12 k1 p1 p21 (p1 k1 p1 p1) p21 (p1 k1 p1 p1) p21 p1 k1

R13 k1 p1 k19 (k2tog yo yo k2tog) k2 (k1 k2tog yo k1 yo k2tog k1) repeat ( ) two more times, k2 (k2tog yo yo k2tog) k19 p1 k1

R14 k1 p1 k19 (p1 k1 p1 p1) p2 (p2tog yrn p3 yrn p2tog) repeat ( ) two more times, p2 (p1 k1 p1 p1) p19 p1 k1

R15 k1 p1 k17 (k2tog yo yo k2tog) k4 (k7) repeat ( ) two more times, k4 (k2tog yo yo k2tog) k17 p1 k1

R16 k1 p1 k17 (p1 k1 p1 p1) p4 (p1 yrn p2tog yrn p3tog yrn p1) repeat ( ) two more times, p4 (p1 k1 p1 p1) p17 p1 k1

R17 k1 p1 k15 (k2tog yo yo k2tog) k6 (k7) repeat ( ) two more times, k6 (k2tog yo yo k2tog) k15 p1 k1

R18 k1 p1 k15 (p1 k1 p1 p1) p6 (p2 yrn p3tog yrn p2) repeat ( ) two more times, p6 (p1 k1 p1 p1) p15 p1 k1

R19 k1 p1 k13 (k2tog yo yo k2tog) k37 (k2tog yo yo k2tog) k13 p1 k1

R20 k1 p1 k13 (p1 k1 p1 p1) p37 (p1 k1 p1 p1) p13 p1 k1

R21 k1 p1 k11 (k2tog yo yo k2tog) k10 (k1 k2tog yo k1 yo k2tog k1) repeat ( ) two more times, k10 (k2tog yo yo k2tog) k11 p1 k1

R22 k1 p1 k11 (p1 k1 p1 p1) p10 (p2tog yrn p3 yrn p2tog) repeat ( ) two more times, p10 (p1 k1 p1 p1) p11 p1 k1

R23 k1 p1 k9 (k2tog yo yo k2tog) k12 (k7) repeat ( ) two more times, k12 (k2tog yo yo k2tog) k9 p1 k1

R24 k1 p1 p9 (p1 k1 p1 p1) p12 (p1 yrn p2tog yrn p3tog yrn p1) repeat ( ) two more times, p12 (p1 k1 p1 p1) p9 p1 k1

R25 k1 p1 k7 (k2tog yo yo k2tog) k14 (k7) repeat ( ) two more times, k14 (k2tog yo yo k2tog) k7 p1 k1

R26 k1 p1 p7 (p1 k1 p1 p1) p14 (p2 yrn p3tog yrn p2) repeat ( ) two more times, p14 (p1 k1 p1 p1) p7 p1 k1

R27 k1 p1 k5 (k2tog yo yo k2tog) k53 (k2tog yo yo k2tog) k5 p1 k1

R28 k1 p1 p5 (p1 k1 p1 p1) p53 (p1 k1 p1 p1) p5 p1 k1

R29 k1 p1 k3 (k2tog yo yo k2tog) k11 (k1 k2tog yo k1 yo k2tog k1) repeat ( ) four more times, k11 (k2tog yo yo k2tog) k3 p1 k1

R30 k1 p1 p3 (p1 k1 p1 p1) p11 (p2tog yrn p3 yrn p2tog) repeat ( ) four more times, p11 (p1 k1 p1 p1) p3 p1 k1

R31 k1 p1 k1 (k2tog yo yo k2tog) k13 (k7) repeat ( ) four more times, k13 (k2tog yo yo k2tog) k1 p1 k1

R32 k1 p1 p1 (p1 k1 p1 p1) p13 (p1 yrn p2tog yrn p3tog yrn p1) repeat ( ) four more times, p13 (p1 k1 p1 p1) p1 p1 k1

R33 k1 p1 k1 (k2tog yo yo k2tog) k13 (k7) repeat ( ) four more times, k13 (k2tog yo yo k2tog) k1 p1 k1

R34 k1 p1 p1 (p1 k1 p1 p1) p13 (p2 yrn p3tog yrn p2) repeat ( ) four more times, p13 (p1 k1 p1 p1) p1 p1 k1

R35 k1 p1 k3 (k2tog yo yo k2tog) k57 (k2tog yo yo k2tog) k3 p1 k1

R36 k1 p1 p3 (p1 k1 p1 p1) p57 (p1 k1 p1 p1) p3 p1 k1

R37 k1 p1 k5 (k2tog yo yo k2tog) k16 (k1 k2tog yo k1 yo k2tog k1) repeat ( ) two more times, k16 (k2tog yo yo k2tog) k5 p1 k1

R38 k1 p1 p5 (p1 k1 p1 p1) p16 (p2tog yrn p3 yrn p2tog) repeat ( ) two more times, p16 (p1 k1 p1 p1) p5 p1 k1

R39 k1 p1 k7 (k2tog yo yo k2tog) k14 (k7) repeat ( ) two more times, k14 (k2tog yo yo k2tog) k7 p1 k1

R40 k1 p1 p7 (p1 k1 p1 p1) p14 (p1 yrn p2tog yrn p3tog yrn p1) repeat ( ) two more times, p14 (p1 k1 p1 p1) p7 p1 k1

R41 k1 p1 k9 (k2tog yo yo k2tog) k12 (k7) repeat ( ) two more times, k12 (k2tog yo yo k2tog) k9 p1 k1

R42 k1 p1 p9 (p1 k1 p1 p1) p12 (p2 yrn p3tog yrn p2) repeat ( ) two more times, p12 (p1 k1 p1 p1) p9 p1 k1

R43 k1 p1 k11 (k2tog yo yo k2tog) k41 (k2tog yo yo k2tog) k11 p1 k1

R44 k1 p1 p11 (p1 k1 p1 p1) p41 (p1 k1 p1 p1) p11 p1 k1

R45 k1 p1 k13 (k2tog yo yo k2tog) k8 (k1 k2tog yo k1 yo k2tog k1) repeat ( ) two more times, k8 (k2tog yo yo k2tog) k13 p1 k1

R46 k1 p1 p13 (p1 k1 p1 p1) p8 (p2tog yrn p3 yrn p2tog) repeat ( ) two more times, p8 (p1 k1 p1 p1) p13 p1 k1

R47 k1 p1 k15 (k2tog yo yo k2tog) k6 (k7) repeat ( ) two more times, k6 (k2tog yo yo k2tog) k15 p1 k1

R48 k1 p1 p15 (p1 k1 p1 p1) p6 (p1 yrn p2tog yrn p3tog yrn p1) repeat ( ) two more times, p6 (p1 k1 p1 p1) p15 p1 k1

R49 k1 p1 k17 (k2tog yo yo k2tog) k4 (k7) repeat ( ) two more times, k4 (k2tog yo yo k2tog) k17 p1 k1

R50 k1 p1 p17 (p1 k1 p1 p1) p4 (p2 yrn p3tog yrn p2) repeat ( ) two more times, p4 (p1 k1 p1 p1) p17 p1 k1

R51 k1 p1 k19 (k2tog yo yo k2tog) k25 (k2tog yo yo k2tog) k19 p1 k1
R52 k1 p1 p19 (p1 k1 p1 p1) p25 (p1 k1 p1 p1) p19 p1 k1
R53 k1 p1 k21 (k2tog yo yo k2tog) k7 (k1 k2tog yo k1 yo k2tog k1) k7 (k2tog yo yo k2tog) k21 p1 k1
R54 k1 p1 p21 (p1 k1 p1 p1) p7 (p2tog yrn p3 yrn p2tog) p7 (p1 k1 p1 p1) p21 p1 k1
R55 k1 p1 k23 (k2tog yo yo k2tog) k5 (k7) k5 (k2tog yo yo k2tog) k23 p1 k1
R56 k1 p1 p23 (p1 k1 p1 p1) p5 (p1 yrn p2tog yrn p3tog yrn p1) p5 (p1 k1 p1 p1) p23 p1 k1
R57 k1 p1 k25 (k2tog yo yo k2tog) k3 (k7) k3 (k2tog yo yo k2tog) k25 p1 k1
R58 k1 p1 p25 (p1 k1 p1 p1) p3 (p2 yrn p3tog yrn p2) p3 (p1 k1 p1 p1) p25 p1 k1

R59 k1 p1 k27 (k2tog yo yo k2tog) k9 (k2tog yo yo k2tog) k27 p1 k1
R60 k1 p1 p27 (p1 k1 p1 p1) p9 (p1 k1 p1 p1) p27 p1 k1
R61 k1 p1 k29 (k2tog yo yo k2tog) k5 (k2tog yo yo k2tog) k29 p1 k1
R62 k1 p1 p29 (p1 k1 p1 p1) p5 (p1 k1 p1 p1) p29 p1 k1
R63 k1 p1 k31 (k2tog yo yo k2tog) k1 (k2tog yo yo k2tog) k31 p1 k1
R64 k1 p1 p31 (p1 k1 p1 p1) p1 (p1 k1 p1 p1) p31 p1 k1

LEFT FRONT SECTION

REPEAT MEDALLION

REPEAT 1-SHETLAND TWIN SECTION WITH EYELID ON EACH SIDE

REPEAT 3-SHETLAND TWIN SECTION WITH EYELID ON EACH SIDE

REPEAT 5-SHETLAND TWIN SECTION 3 TIMES

Knit one row
Bo all sts

Lace Wrap 2

MATERIALS
• 6 balls Patons Silk Bamboo Yarn, Plum. 65g ball (93 m/ 102 yd)

NEEDLES
• US 10 (6 mm), US 10 cable needle, needle for weaving ends

SIZE
• 80" (62") x 15". The shorter (62") wrap is produced by starting at R41 using one ball less

Instructions

There are 60 sts on this wrap, with a center section of three cables.

Co 60 sts
Knit one row

BEGINNING SECTION

5-MOTIFS
R1 k1 p1 (k2 k2 k2tog yo yo k2tog k2 k1) repeat ( ) four more times, k1 p1 k1

R2 k1 p1 k1 (k1 k2 k1, k1 p1 into yos, k1 k2 k2) repeat ( ) four more times, p1 k1

R3 k1 p1 (k2 k2tog yo yo k2tog k2tog yo yo k2tog k1) repeat ( ) four more times, k1 p1 k1

R4 k1 p1 k1 (k1 k1, k1 p1 into yos, k1 k1, k1 p1 into yos, k1 k2) repeat ( ) four more times, p1 k1

R5 repeat R1

R6 repeat R2

R7 k1 p1 k56 p1 k1

R8 repeat R7

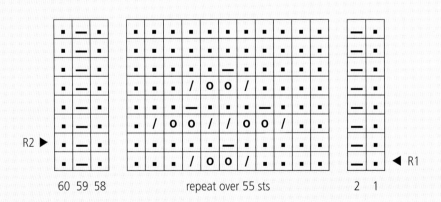

Chart of the 5-motif section. For the 3-motif and 1-motif sections,
replace the outer repeats with k11 and k22 respectively.

R9-R16 repeat R1-R8

(continued on page 92)

(continued from page 90)

3-MOTIFS

R17 k1 p1 k11 (k2 k2 k2tog yo yo k2tog k2 k1) repeat ( ) two more times, k11 k1 p1 k1

R18 k1 p1 k1 k11 (k1 k2 k1, k1 p1 into yos, k1 k2 k2) repeat ( ) two more times, k11 p1 k1

R19 k1 p1 k11 (k2 k2tog yo yo k2tog k2tog yo yo k2tog k1) repeat ( ) two more times, k11 k1 p1 k1

R20 k1 p1 k1 k11 (k1 k1, k1 p1 into yos, k1 k1, k1 p1 into yos, k1 k1) repeat ( ) two more times, k11 p1 k1

R21 repeat R17

R22 repeat R18

R23 k1 p1 k56 p1 k1

R24 repeat R23

R25-R32 repeat R17-R24

1-MOTIF

R33 k1 p1 k22 (k2 k2 k2tog yo yo k2tog k2 k1) k22 k1 p1 k1

R34 k1 p1 k1 k22 (k1 k2 k1, k1 p1 into yos, k1 k2 k2) k22 p1 k1

R35 k1 p1 k22 (k2 k2tog yo yo k2tog k2tog yo yo k2tog k1) k22 k1 p1 k1

R36 k1 p1 k1 k22 (k1 k1, k1 p1 into yos, k1 k1, k1 p1 into yos, k1 k1) k22 p1 k1

R37 repeat R33

R38 repeat R34

R39 k1 p1 k56 p1 k1

R40 repeat R39

R41-R56 repeat R33-R40 two more times

Reverse pattern (R57-R88)

Repeat R17-R32

Repeat R1-R16

MIDDLE SECTION

See charts on pages 93-94.

R1 k1 p1 k24 (k2tog yo yo k2tog) (k2tog yo yo k2tog) k24 p1 k1

R2 k1 p1 k24 (k1, k1 p1 into yos, k1) (k1, k1 p1 into yos, k1) k24 p1 k1

R3 k1 p1 k22 (k2tog yo yo k2tog) k4 (k2tog yo yo k2tog) k22 p1 k1

R4 k1 p1 k22 (k1, k1 p1 into yos, k1) k4 (k1, k1 p1 into yos, k1) k22 p1 k1

R5 k1 p1 k20 (k2tog yo yo k2tog) k8 (k2tog yo yo k2tog) k20 p1 k1

R6 k1 p1 k20 (k1, k1 p1 into yos, k1) k8 (k1, k1 p1 into yos, k1) k20 p1 k1

R7 k1 p1 k18 (k2tog yo yo k2tog) k2 (k2 k2tog yo yo k2tog k2) k2 (k2tog yo yo k2tog) k18 p1 k1

R8 k1 p1 k18 (k1, k1 p1 into yos, k1) k2 (k2 k1, k1 p1 into yos, k1 k2) k2 (k1, k1 p1 into yos, k1) k18 p1 k1

R9 k1 p1 k16 (k2tog yo yo k2tog) k4 (k2tog yo yo k2tog) (k2tog yo yo k2tog) k4 (k2tog yo yo k2tog) k16 p1 k1

R10 k1 p1 k16 (k1, k1 p1 into yos, k1) k4 (k1, k1 p1 into yos, k1) (k1, k1 p1 into yos, k1) k4 (k1, k1 p1 into yos, k1) k16 p1 k1

R11 k1 p1 k14 (k2tog yo yo k2tog) k6 (k2 k2tog yo yo k2tog k2) k6 (k2tog yo yo k2tog) k14 p1 k1

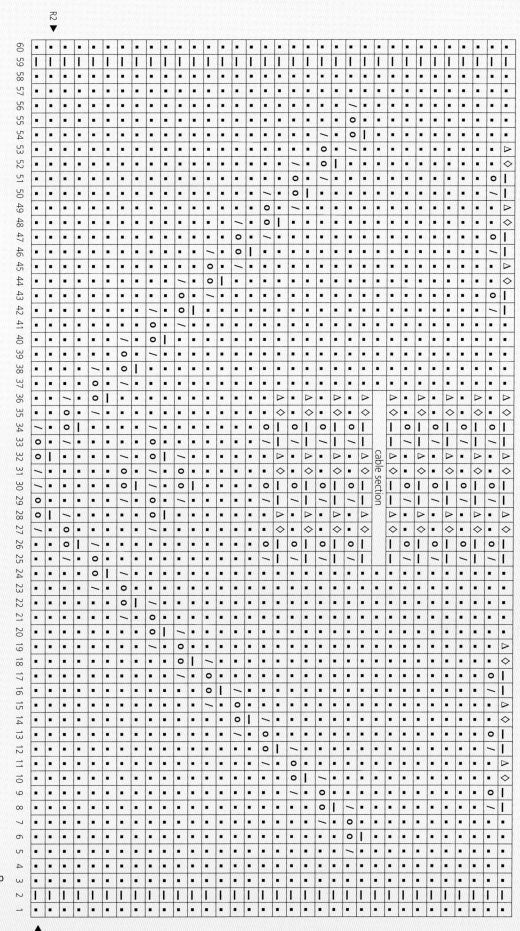

Chart of start of middle section up
to the beginning of the 3-Cable
section

Chart of completion of the middle
section from the end of the 3-Cable
section

cable section

R12 k1 p1 k14 (k1, k1 p1 into yos, k1) k6 (k2 k1, k1 p1 into yos, k1 k2) k6 (k1, k1 p1 into yos, k1) k14 p1 k1

R13 k1 p1 k12 (k2tog yo yo k2tog) k24 (k2tog yo yo k2tog) k12 p1 k1

R14 k1 p1 k12 (k1, k1 p1 into yos, k1) k24 (k1, k1 p1 into yos, k1) k12 p1 k1

R15 k1 p1 k10 (k2tog yo yo k2tog) k28 (k2tog yo yo k2tog) k10 p1 k1

R16 k1 p1 k10 (k1, k1 p1 into yos, k1) k28 (k1, k1 p1 into yos, k1) k10 p1 k1

CENTER CABLE START, LACE HOLES

R17 k1 p1 k8 (k2tog yo yo k2tog) k10 (k2tog yo k2) repeat ( ) two more times, k10 (k2tog yo yo k2tog) k8 p1 k1

R18 k1 p1 k8 (k1, k1 p1 into yos, k1) k10 (p2tog yrn p2) repeat ( ) two more times, k10 (k1, k1 p1 into yos, k1) k8 p1 k1

R19 k1 p1 k6 (k2tog yo yo k2tog) k12 (k2tog yo k2) repeat ( ) two more times, k12 (k2tog yo yo k2tog) k6 p1 k1

R20 k1 p1 k6 (k1, k1 p1 into yos, k1) k12 (p2tog yrn p2) repeat ( ) two more times, k12 (k1, k1 p1 into yos, k1) k6 p1 k1

R21 k1 p1 k4 (k2tog yo yo k2tog) k14 (k2tog yo k2) repeat ( ) two more times, k14 (k2tog yo yo k2tog) k4 p1 k1

R22 k1 p1 k4 (k1, k1 p1 into yos, k1) k14 (p2tog yrn p2) repeat ( ) two more times, k14 (k1, k1 p1 into yos, k1) k4 p1 k1

R23 k1 p1 k2 (k2tog yo yo k2tog) k16 (k2tog yo k2) repeat ( ) two more times, k16 (k2tog yo yo k2tog) k2 p1 k1

R24 k1 p1 k2 (k1, k1 p1 into yos, k1) k16 (p2tog yrn p2) repeat ( ) two more times, k16 (k1, k1 p1 into yos, k1) k2 p1 k1

CENTER CABLE CONTINATION, NO LACE HOLES

R25 k1 p1 k22 (k2tog yo k1, slip the next 3 sts onto cable needle and hold at back of work, k1 k2tog from left hand needle, yo, k2 from the cable needle, knit next st on left hand needle and last st on cable needle together, yo k2) k22 p1 k1

R26 k1 p1 k22 (p2tog yrn p2) repeat ( ) two more times, k22 p1 k1

R27 k1 p1 k22 (k2tog yo k2) repeat ( ) two more times, k22 p1 k1

R28 k1 p1 k22 (p2tog yrn p2) repeat ( ) two more times, k22 p1 k1

R29 k1 p1 k22 (k2tog yo k2) repeat ( ) two more times, k22 p1 k1

R30 k1 p1 k22 (p2tog yrn p2) repeat ( ) two more times, k22 p1 k1

R31 k1 p1 k22 (k2tog yo k2) repeat ( ) two more times, k22 p1 k1

R32 k1 p1 k22 (p2tog yrn p2) repeat ( ) two more times, k22 p1 k1

3-CABLE SECTION

R33 k1 p1 *k5 (k2tog yo k2) repeat ( ) two more times *, repeat * to * two more times, k5 p1 k1

R34 k1 p1 k5 *(p2tog yrn p2) repeat ( ) two more times k5*, repeat * to * two more times, p1 k1

R35 k1 p1 *k5 (k2tog yo k2) repeat ( ) two more times *, repeat * to * two more times, k5 p1 k1

R36 k1 p1 k5 *(p2tog yrn p2) repeat ( ) two more times k5*, repeat * to * two more times, p1 k1

R37 k1 p1 *k5 (k2tog yo k2) repeat ( ) two more times *, repeat * to * two more times, k5 p1 k1

R38 k1 p1 k5 *(p2tog yrn p2) repeat ( ) two more times k5*, repeat * to * two more times, p1 k1

R39 k1 p1 *k5 (k2tog yo k2) repeat ( ) two more times *, repeat * to * two more times, k5 p1 k1

R40 k1 p1 k5 *(p2tog yrn p2) repeat ( ) two more times k5*, repeat * to * two more times, p1 k1

R41 k1 p1 *k5 (k2tog yo k1, slip the next 3 sts onto cable needle and hold at back of work, k1 k2tog from main needle, yo, k2 from the cable needle, knit next st on main needle and last st on cable needle together, yo k2)*, repeat * to * two more times, k5 p1 k1

R42 k1 p1 k5 *(p2tog yrn p2) repeat ( ) two more times k5*, repeat * to * two more times, p1 k1

R43 k1 p1 *k5 (k2tog yo k2) repeat ( ) two more times *, repeat * to * two more times, k5 p1 k1

R44 k1 p1 k5 *(p2tog yrn p2) repeat ( ) two more times k5*, repeat * to * two more times, p1 k1

R45 k1 p1 *k5 (k2tog yo k2) repeat ( ) two more times *, repeat * to * two more times, k5 p1 k1

R46 k1 p1 k5 *(p2tog yrn p2) repeat ( ) two more times k5*, repeat * to * two more times, p1 k1

R47 k1 p1 *k5 (k2tog yo k2) repeat ( ) two more times *, repeat * to * two more times, k5 p1 k1

R48 k1 p1 k5 *(p2tog yrn p2) repeat ( ) two more times k5*, repeat * to * two more times, p1 k1

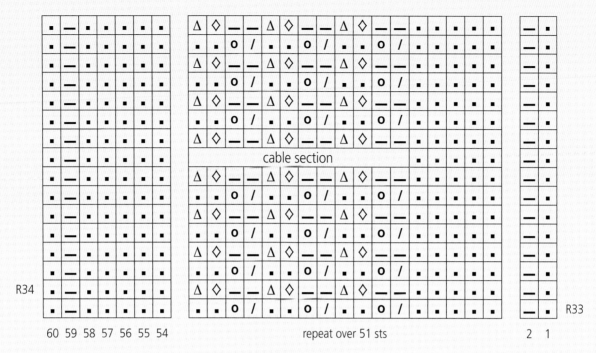

R34

60 59 58 57 56 55 54   repeat over 51 sts   2 1

Chart of 3-Cable section

R49-R112: repeat R33-R48 four more times

CENTER CABLE CONTINATION, NO LACE HOLES

R113 k1 p1 k22 (k2tog yo k2) repeat ( ) two more times, k22 p1 k1

R114 k1 p1 k22 (p2tog yrn p2) repeat ( ) two more times, k22 p1 k1

R115 k1 p1 k22 (k2tog yo k2) repeat ( ) two more times, k22 p1 k1

R116 k1 p1 k22 (p2tog yrn p2) repeat ( ) two more times, k22 p1 k1

R117 k1 p1 k22 (k2tog yo k2) repeat ( ) two more times, k22 p1 k1

R118 k1 p1 k22 (p2tog yrn p2) repeat ( ) two more times, k22 p1 k1

R119 k1 p1 k22 (k2tog yo k2) repeat ( ) two more times, k22 p1 k1

R120 k1 p1 k22 (p2tog yrn p2) repeat ( ) two more times, k22 p1 k1

CENTER CABLE END, LACE HOLES

R121 k1 p1 k2 (k2tog yo yo k2tog) k16 (k2tog yo k1, slip the next 3 sts onto cable needle and hold at back of work, k1 k2tog from left hand needle, yo, k2 from the cable needle, knit next st on left hand needle and last st on cable needle together, yo k2) k16 (k2tog yo yo k2tog) k2 p1 k1

R122 k1 p1 k2 (k1, k1 p1 into yos, k1) k16 (p2tog yrn p2) repeat ( ) two more times, k16 (k1, k1 p1 into yos, k1) k2 p1 k1

R123 k1 p1 k4 (k2tog yo yo k2tog) k14 (k2tog yo k2) repeat ( ) two more times, k14 (k2tog yo yo k2tog) k4 p1 k1

R124 k1 p1 k4 (k1, k1 p1 into yos, k1) k14 (p2tog yrn p2) repeat ( ) two more times, k14 (k1, k1 p1 into yos, k1) k4 p1 k1

R125 k1 p1 k6 (k2tog yo yo k2tog) k12 (k2tog yo k2) repeat ( ) two more times, k12 (k2tog yo yo k2tog) k6 p1 k1

R126 k1 p1 k6 (k1, k1 p1 into yos, k1) k12 (p2tog yrn p2) repeat ( ) two more times, k12 (k1, k1 p1 into yos, k1) k6 p1 k1

R127 k1 p1 k8 (k2tog yo yo k2tog) k10 (k2tog yo k2) repeat ( ) two more times, k10 (k2tog yo yo k2tog) k8 p1 k1

R128 k1 p1 k8 (k1, k1 p1 into yos, k1) k10 (p2tog yrn p2) repeat ( ) two more times, k10 (k1, k1 p1 into yos, k1) k8 p1 k1

COMPLETION OF MIDDLE SECTION

R129 k1 p1 k10 (k2tog yo yo k2tog) k28 (k2tog yo yo k2tog) k10 p1 k1

R130 k1 p1 k10 (k1, k1 p1 into yos, k1) k28 (k1, k1 p1 into yos, k1) k10 p1 k1

R131 k1 p1 k12 (k2tog yo yo k2tog) k24 (k2tog yo yo k2tog) k12 p1 k1

R132 k1 p1 k12 (k1, k1 p1 into yos, k1) k24 (k1, k1 p1 into yos, k1) k12 p1 k1

R133 k1 p1 k14 (k2tog yo yo k2tog) k6 (k2 k2tog yo yo k2tog k2) k6 (k2tog yo yo k2tog) k14 p1 k1

R134 k1 p1 k14 (k1, k1 p1 into yos, k1) k6 (k2 k1, k1 p1 into yos, k1 k2) k6 (k1, k1 p1 into yos, k1) k14 p1 k1

R135 k1 p1 k16 (k2tog yo yo k2tog) k4 (k2tog yo yo k2tog) (k2tog yo yo k2tog) k4 (k2tog yo yo k2tog) k16 p1 k1

R136 k1 p1 k16 (k1, k1 p1 into yos, k1) k4 (k1, k1 p1 into yos, k1) (k1, k1 p1 into yos, k1) k4 (k1, k1 p1 into yos, k1) k16 p1 k1

R137 k1 p1 k18 (k2tog yo yo k2tog) k2 (k2 k2tog yo yo k2tog k2) k2 (k2tog yo yo k2tog) k18 p1 k1

R138 k1 p1 k18 (k1, k1 p1 into yos, k1) k2 (k2 k1, k1 p1 into yos, k1 k2) k2 (k1, k1 p1 into yos, k1) k18 p1 k1

R139 k1 p1 k20 (k2tog yo yo k2tog) k8 (k2tog yo yo k2tog) k20 p1 k1

R140 k1 p1 k20 (k1, k1 p1 into yos, k1) k8 (k1, k1 p1 into yos, k1) k20 p1 k1

R141 k1 p1 k22 (k2tog yo yo k2tog) k4 (k2tog yo yo k2tog) k22 p1 k1

R142 k1 p1 k22 (k1, k1 p1 into yos, k1) k4 (k1, k1 p1 into yos, k1) k22 p1 k1

R143 k1 p1 k24 (k2tog yo yo k2tog) (k2tog yo yo k2tog) k24 p1 k1

R144 k1 p1 k24 (k1, k1 p1 into yos, k1) (k1, k1 p1 into yos, k1) k24 p1 k1

R145 k1 p1 k56 p1 k1

R146 k1 p1 k56 p1 k1

END SECTION

Repeat Beginning Section R1-R86 (R41-R86 for shorter wrap)

Knit one row

Bo all sts

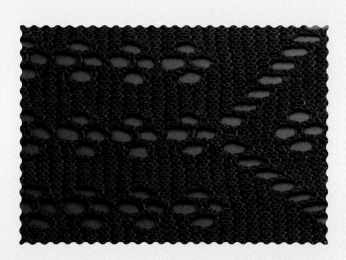

SHAWLS

• Shawls have been part of clothing for centuries, including baby shawls, working shawls and decorative shawls. They are part of traditional dress in many countries, and this is often reflected in the design, shape and pattern stitches used, representing not only the countries but family histories.

• Shawls not only provide warmth, comfort and intrigue, but with today's new yarns, they can also dazzle and shimmer. They can be constructed in various ways: a square centre with four borders, circular, point to point, triangular, and mirror are just some of the methods I use. Shawls which are knitted in garter st look the same when viewed from either side.

• Shawls are wonderful to both give and receive at any stage in your life.

Reversible Shawl

MATERIALS
• Four balls Patons Silk Bamboo Yarn, Stone. 65g ball (93 m/ 102 yd)

NEEDLES
• US 10 (6 mm) needles, needle to weave ends

SIZE
• 48" x 32"

Instructions

This triangular shawl is worked from the bottom to the top. The increase st is worked as a yo and on the return row is knitted as a stitch. It is all garter stitch with a 7-st Circle motif worked over 8 rows, and 5-st separation. It can be worn with either side showing: one side is smooth, the other is slightly more rugged.

BOTTOM OF SHAWL
Co 2 sts

R1 k2
R2 yo k2
R3 yo k3
R4 yo k4
R5 yo k5

(continued on page 100)

(continued from page 98)

R6 yo k6
R7 yo k7
R8 yo k8

FIRST CIRCLE MOTIF
motif stitches in ( )
R1 yo k1 (k1 k2tog yo k1 yo k2togb k1) k1
R2 yo, k to end of row
R3 yo k2 (k2tog yo k3 yo k2tog) k2
R4 yo, k to end of row
R5 yo k3 (k1 yo k2togb k1 k2tog yo k1) k3
R6 yo, k to end of row
R7 yo k4 (k2 yo sskp yo k2) k4
R8 yo, k to end of row

SECOND CIRCLE MOTIF
Repeat first circle motif pattern stitches, with the yos becoming additional k sts.

THIRD CIRCLE MOTIF
Repeat first circle motif pattern stitches, with the yos becoming additional k sts.

Multiple circle motifs

Every 24 rows, an additional column of circle motifs is added to each side of the central motifs, with each column of motifs being separated by 5 k sts. The three columns of motifs start after there are 33 sts on the needle.

THREE COLUMNS OF MOTIFS AND GARTER ST SEPARATION
R1 yo k1 (k1 k2tog yo k1 yo k2togb k1) k5 (k1 k2tog yo k1 yo k2togb k1) k5 (k1 k2tog yo k1 yo k2togb k1) k1 (34 sts)
R2 yo, k to end of row
R3 yo k2 (k2tog yo k3 yo k2tog) k5 (k2tog yo k3 yo k2tog) k5 (k2tog yo k3 yo k2tog) k2
R4 yo, k to end of row
R5 yo k3 (k1 yo k2togb k1 k2tog yo k1) k5 (k1 yo k2togb k1 k2tog yo k1) k5 (k1 yo k2togb k1 k2tog yo k1) k3
R6 yo, k to end of row
R7 yo k4 (k2 yo sskp yo k2) k5 (k2 yo sskp yo k2) k5 (k2 yo sskp yo k2) k4
R8 yo, k to end of row

The chart on page 102 shows the situation at this point.

Second set of motifs: repeat the 3-motif pattern stitches, with the yos becoming additional k sts.

Third set of motifs: repeat 3-motif pattern stitches, with the yos becoming additional k sts.

Continue until there are six columns of motifs on each side of the central column, with the outside columns each consisting of three motifs.

Bo all sts

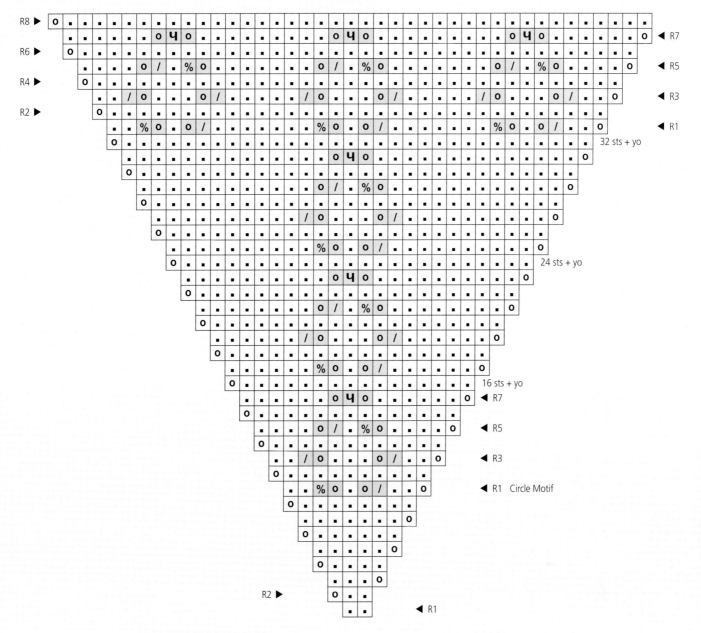

Chart showing motif placement and increases up to the end of the first set of three motifs

Mirror Shawlette

MATERIALS
• 2 balls Patons Silk Bamboo Yarn, Coal. 65g ball (93 m /102 yd)

NEEDLES
• US 10 (6 mm), needle to weave in ends

SIZE
• 58" x 21"

Instructions

See the notes on the Butterfly shawl pattern (page 105).

Co 135 sts, medium-firm co
Knit one row

LACE PEBBLES
R1 k1 (k2tog yo yo k2tog) repeat ( ) 18 more times, **k1** (k2tog yo yo k2tog) repeat ( ) 18 more times, k1
R2 k1 (k1, k1 p1 into yos, k1) repeat ( ) 18 more times, **k1** (k1, k1 p1 into yos, k1) repeat ( ) 18 more times, k1
R3 k1 k2 (k2tog yo yo k2tog) repeat ( ) 17 more times, k2 **k1** k2 (k2tog yo yo k2tog) repeat ( ) 17 more times, k2 k1
R4 k1 k2 (k1, k1 p1 into yos, k1) repeat ( ) 17 more times, k2 **k1** k2 (k1, k1 p1 into yos, k1) repeat ( ) 17 more times, k2 k1

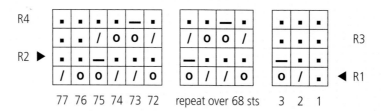

Chart showing Lace Pebbles on right hand side of shawlette

Continue with Part 2 (starting at R89) of the Butterfly shawl pattern.

Butterfly Shawl

MATERIALS
• 10 balls Patons Silk Bamboo Yarn, Coal. 65g ball (93 m /102 yd)

NEEDLES
• US 10 (6 mm), needle to weave in ends

SIZE
• 84" x 42". The Co firmness will affect both the width and depth

Instructions

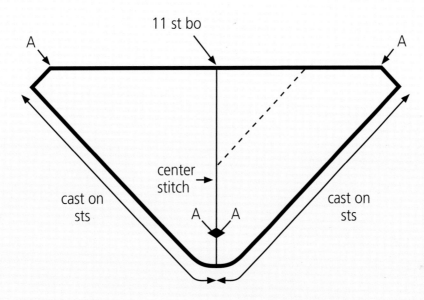

A: start of decrease at outside edge and center line.
Decreases continue in both places on each side until
5 sts remain on each side of the center st

- - - - - - End of Part 1

Diagram of shawl construction. For details see text.

The Shawlette pattern found on page 102 in this book is formed from Part 2 of this shawl.

PART 1

Part 1 has a right hand and left hand section (Sections 1 and 2) Section 1 is worked in five multiples of 24 sts + 13 (133 sts), a k centre st (**k1**), and a second Section of five multiples of 24 sts + 13 (133 sts) for a total of 267 sts.

The shaping which begins on R33 is worked on the outside and inside of both Sections on the RS rows. Once 88 rows have been knitted, the shawl continues with a Part 2, with the shaping continuing as before until the final 11 bo sts at the top centre.

Note that the use of ( ) in Part 1 is different from elsewhere in the book. The total number of times the stitches in the ( ) are repeated is given, with the "repeat" being used in conjunction with the "*" in the pattern.

See charts on pages 108-109.

Co 267 sts quite firmly (see the diagram).
Foundation row: k133, **k1** and place marker on this centre st, k133

R1 [k2 *k2tog yo k4 repeat from * to last 5 sts k2tog yo k3] **k1**, repeat [ ]
R2 and every other row: k all sts on needle
R3 [k1 *k2tog yo k1 yo k2tog k1 repeat from * to centre] **k1**, repeat [ ] to end of row
R5 [k2tog yo *k3 yo k3tog yo repeat from * to last 5 sts k3 yo k2tog] **k1**, repeat [ ]
R7 [k1 *yo k2tog yo k3tog yo k1 repeat from * to centre] **k1**, repeat [ ] to end of row
R9 [k2 *yo k3tog yo k3 repeat from * to last 5 sts yo k3tog yo k2] **k1**, repeat [ ]
R11 [k1 k2tog yo (k1 yo k2tog yo k3tog yo) twice k7 *(yo k2tog yo k3tog yo k1) 3 times k6 repeat from * to last 15 sts (yo k2tog yo k3tog yo k1) twice yo k2tog k1] **k1**, repeat [ ]
R13 [k2tog yo (k3 yo k3tog yo) twice *k2 k2tog yo kl yo k2tog k2 (yo k3tog yo k3) twice yo k3tog yo repeat from * to last 23 sts k2 k2tog yo k1 yo k2tog k2 (yo k3tog yo k3) twice yo k2tog] **k1**, repeat [ ]
R15 [k1 *(yo k2tog yo k3tog yo k1) twice k2 k2tog yo k3 yo k2tog k3 repeat from * to last 12 sts (yo k2tog yo k3tog yo kl) twice] **k1**, repeat [ ]
R17 [k2 *(yo k3tog yo k3) twice (k2tog yo) twice k1 (yo k2tog) twice k3 repeat from * to last 11 sts yo k3tog yo k3 yo k3tog yo k2] **k1**, repeat [ ]
R19 [k1 k2tog yo k1 *yo k2tog yo k3tog yo k4 (k2tog yo) twice k3 (yo k2tog) twice k4 repeat from * to last 9 sts yo k2tog yo k3tog yo k1 yo k2tog k1] **k1**, repeat [ ]
R21 [k2tog yo *k3 yo k3tog yo k4 (k2tog yo) 3 times k1 (yo k2tog) 3 times k1 repeat from * to last 11 sts [k3 yo k3tog yo k3 yo k2tog] **k1**, repeat [ ]
R23 [k1 yo k2tog yo k3tog yo k5 (k2tog yo) 3 times *k3 (yo k2tog) 3 times k3 k2tog yo k4 (k2tog yo) 3 times repeat from * to last 20 sts k3 (yo k2tog) 3 times k5 yo k2tog yo k3tog yo k1] **k1**, repeat [ ]
R25 [k2 yo k3tog yo k5 (k2tog yo) 4 times k1 (yo k2tog) 4 times *k7 (k2tog yo) 4 times k1 (yo k2tog) 4 times repeat from * to last 10 sts k5 yo k3tog yo k2] **k1**, repeat [ ]
R27 [k1 k2tog yo k6 (k2tog yo) 4 times k3 (yo k2tog) 4 times *k1 k2tog yo k2 (k2tog yo) 4 times k3 (yo k2tog) 4 times repeat from * to last 9 sts k6 yo k2tog k1] **k1**, repeat [ ]
R29 [k2tog yo k6 *(k2tog yo) 5 times k1 (yo k2tog) 5 times k3 repeat from * to last 5 sts k3 yo k2tog] **k1**, repeat [ ]
R31 [k7 *(k2tog yo) 5 times k3 (yo k2tog) 5 times k1 repeat from * to last 6 sts k6] **k1**, repeat [ ]
R33 [k1 k2tog k5 *(k2tog yo) 5 times k1 (yo k2tog) 5 times k3 repeat from * to last 5 sts k2 k2tog kl (131 sts)] **k1**, repeat [ ]
R35 [k1 k2tog k5 *(k2tog yo) 4 times k3 (yo k2tog) 4 times k5 repeat from * to last 3 sts k2tog k1 (129 sts)] **k1**, repeat [ ]
R37 [k1 k2tog k5 *(k2tog yo) 4 times k1 (yo k2tog) 4 times k1 k2tog yo k1 yo k2tog k1 repeat from * to last 25 sts (k2tog yo) 4 times k1 (yo k2tog) 4 times k5 k2tog k1 (127 sts)] **k1**, repeat [ ]

R39 [k1 k2tog k5 *(k2tog yo) 3 times k3 (yo k2tog) 3 times k1 k2tog yo k3 yo k2tog k1 repeat from * to last 23 sts (k2tog yo) 3 times k3 (yo k2tog) 3 times k5 k2tog k1 (125 sts)] **k1**, repeat [ ]

R41 [k1 k2tog k5 *(k2tog yo) 3 times k1 (yo k2tog) 3 times k1 (k2tog yo) twice k1 (yo k2tog) twice k1 repeat from * to last 21 sts (k2tog yo) 3 times k1 (yo k2tog) 3 times k5 k2tog kl (123 sts)] **k1**, repeat [ ]

R43 [k1 k2tog k5 *(k2tog yo) twice k3 (yo k2tog) twice k1 repeat from * to last 7 sts k4 k2tog k1 (121 sts)] **k1**, repeat [ ]

R45 [k1 k2tog k5 *(k2tog yo) twice k1 (yo k2tog) twice **k1** (k2tog yo) 3 times k1 (yo k2tog) 3 times k1 repeat from * to last 17 sts (k2tog yo) twice k1 (yo k2tog) twice k5 k2tog k1 (119 sts)] **k1**, repeat [ ]

R47 [k1 k2tog k5 *k2tog yo k3 yo k2tog k1 (k2tog yo) 3 times k3 (yo k2tog) 3 times k1 repeat from * to last 15 sts k2tog yo k3 yo k2tog k5 k2tog k1 (117 sts)] **k1**, repeat [ ]

R49 [k1 k2tog k5 *k2tog yo k1 yo k2tog k1 (k2tog yo) 4 times k1 (yo k2tog) 4 times k1 repeat from * to last 13 sts k2tog yo k1 yo k2tog k5 k2tog k1 (115 sts)] **k1**, repeat [ ]

R51 k1 k2tog k6 *yo k2tog k1 (k2tog yo) 4 times k3 (yo k2tog) 4 times k2 repeat from * to last 34 sts yo k2tog k1 (k2tog yo) 4 times k3 (yo k2tog) 4 times k1 k2tog yo k6 k2tog k1 (113 sts)] **k1**, repeat [ ]

R53 [k1 k2tog k7 *(k2tog yo) 5 times k1 (yo k2tog) 5 times k3 repeat from * to last 7 sts k4 k2tog kl (111 sts)] **k1**, repeat [ ]

R55 [kl k2tog k5 *(k2tog yo) 5 times k3 (yo k2tog) 5 times k1 repeat from * to last 7 sts k4 k2tog k1 (109 sts)] **k1**, repeat [ ]

R57 [k1 k2tog k5 *(k2tog yo) 5 times k1 (yo k2tog) 5 times k3 repeat from * to last 5 sts k2 k2tog k1 (107 sts)] **k1**, repeat [ ]

R59 [k1 k2tog k5 *(k2tog yo) 4 times k3 (yo k2tog) 4 times k2 yo k2tog k1 repeat from * to last 27 sts (k2tog yo) 4 times k3 (yo k2tog) 4 times k5 k2tog k1 (105 sts)] **k1**, repeat [ ]

R61 [k1 k2tog k5 *(k2tog yo) 4 times k1 (yo k2tog) 4 times k2 yo k3tog yo k2 repeat from * to last 25 sts (k2tog yo) 4 times k1 (yo k2tog) 4 times k5 k2tog k1 (103 sts)] **k1**, repeat [ ]

R63 [k1 k2tog k5 *(k2tog yo) 3 times k3 (yo k2tog) 3 times k4 yo k2tog k3 repeat from * to last 23 sts (k2tog yo) 3 times k3 (yo k2tog) 3 times k5 k2tog k1 (101 sts)] **k1**, repeat [ ]

R65 [k1 k2tog k5 *(k2tog yo) 3 times k1 (yo k2tog) 3 times k11 repeat from * to last 21 sts (k2tog yo) 3 times k1 (yo k2tog) 3 times k5 k2tog k1 (99 sts)] **k1**, repeat [ ]

R67 [k1 k2tog k5 *(k2tog yo) twice k3 (yo k2tog) twice k6 yo k2tog k5 repeat from * to last 19 sts (k2tog yo) twice k3 (yo k2tog) twice k5 k2tog k1 (97 sts)] **k1**, repeat [ ]

R69 [k1 k2tog k5 *(k2tog yo) twice k1 (yo k2tog) twice k5 k2tog yo k1 yo k2tog k5 repeat from * to last 17 sts (k2tog yo) twice k1 (yo k2tog) twice k5 k2tog k1 (95 sts)] **k1**, repeat [ ]

R71 [k1 k2tog k5 *k2tog yo k3 yo k2tog k5 repeat from * to last 3 sts k2tog k1 (93 sts)] **k1**, repeat [ ]

R73 [k1 k2tog k5 *k2tog yo k1 yo k2tog k4 k2tog yo k1 yo k2tog yo k3tog yo k1 yo k2tog k4 repeat from * to last 13 sts k2tog yo k1 yo k2tog k5 k2tog k1 (91 sts)] **k1**, repeat [ ]

R75 [k1 k2tog k5 *k2tog yo k5 k2tog yo k3 yo k3tog yo k3 yo k2tog k4 repeat from * to last 11 sts k2tog yo k6 k2tog k1 (89 sts)] **k1**, repeat [ ]

R77 [k1 k2tog k9 *k2tog yo (k1 yo k2tog yo k3tog yo) twice k1 yo k2tog k7 repeat from * to last 5 sts k2 k2tog k1 (87 sts)] **k1**, repeat [ ]

R79 [k1 k2tog k7 *k2tog yo (k3 yo k3tog yo) twice k3 yo k2tog k5 repeat from * to last 5 sts k2 k2tog k1 (85 sts)] **k1**, repeat [ ]

R81 [k1 k2tog k4 *k2tog yo (k1 yo k2tog yo k3tog yo) 3 times k1 yo k2tog k1 repeat from * to last 6 sts k3 k2tog k1 (83 sts)] **k1**, repeat [ ]

R83 [k1 k2tog k2 k2tog *yo k3 yo k3tog repeat from * to last 10 sts yo k3 yo k2tog k2 k2tog k1 (81 sts)] **k1**, repeat [ ]

R85 [k1 k2tog k2 *yo k2tog yo k3tog yo k1 repeat from * to last 4 sts k1 k2tog k1 (79 sts)] **k1**, repeat [ ]

R87 [k1 k2tog k2 *yo k3tog yo k3 repeat from * to last 8 sts yo k3tog yo k2 k2tog k1 (77 sts)] **k1**, repeat [ ]

R88 k

Chart showing the first R1–R50 of the right-hand half of the shawl.
The sts included in the repeats specified by the * are shaded.

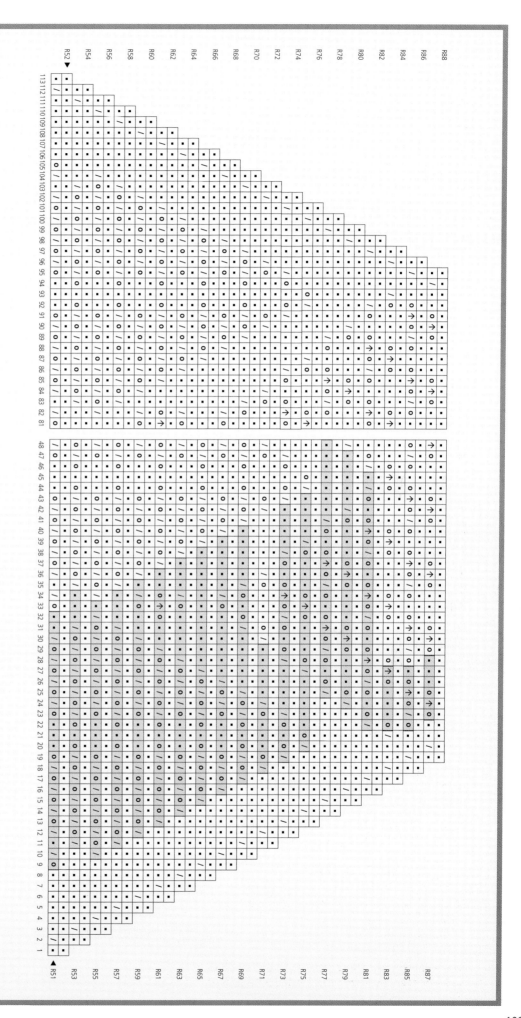

Chart showing R51-R88 of the right-hand half of the shawl. The sts included in the repeats specified by the * are shaded.

PART 2

Part 1, Section 1 ends with 77 sts, centre st (**k1**), then Section 2 with 77 sts

In Part 2, all sts for the row on both sides of the center st are provided.

SEPARATION ROWS

R89 k1 k2tog k71 k2tog k1 **k1** k1 k2tog k71 k2tog k1 (75 sts)

R90 k

Note on Vandyke pattern

Chart showing the stitch usage in the Vandyke pattern. The k3tog and the stitches it uses are in grey, while the "k1 p1 k1 into next st" and the stitch in the row below into which the stitches are knitted are shown in yellow.

VANDYKE

R91 k1 k2tog k1 (k3tog, k1 p1 k1 into next st) repeat ( ) 16 more times, k2tog k1 **k1** k1 k2tog k1 (k3tog, k1 p1 k1 into next st) repeat ( ) 16 more times, k2tog k1

R92 k

R93 k1 k2tog (k1 p1 k1 into next st, k3tog) repeat ( ) 15 more times, k1 p1 k1 into next st, k4tog k1 **k1** k1 k2tog (k1 p1 k1 into next st, k3tog) repeat ( ) 15 more times, k1 p1 k1 into next st, k4tog k1

R94 k

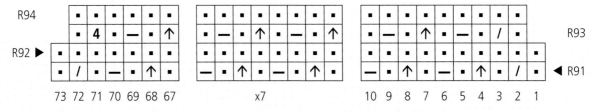

Chart of the Vandyke pattern in rows 91-94 on the right hand side of the shawl

---

SEPARATION ROWS

R95 k1 k2tog k65 k2tog k1 **k1** k1 k2tog k65 k2tog

R96 k

MEDALLION

R97 k1 k2tog k2 (k3 k2tog yo k1 yo skp k3 k1) repeat ( ) four more times, k1 k2tog k1 **k1** k1 k2tog k2 (k3 k2tog yo k1 yo skp k3 k1) repeat ( ) four more times, k1 k2tog k1

R98 k3 (k3 k2togb yo k3 yo k2tog k2) repeat ( ) four more times, k4 **k1** k3 (k3 k2togb yo k3 yo k2tog k2)repeat ( ) four more times, k4

R99 k1 k2tog k1 (k1 k2tog yo k2tog yo k1 yo skp yo skp k1 k1) repeat ( ) four more times, k2tog k1 **k1** k1 k2tog k1 (k1 k2tog yo k2tog yo k1 yo skp yo skp k1 k1) repeat ( ) four more times, k2tog k1

R100 k2 (k1 k2togb yo k2togb yo k3 yo k2tog yo k2tog) repeat ( ) four more times, k3 **k1** k2 (k1 k2togb yo k2togb yo k3 yo k2tog yo k2tog) repeat ( ) four more times, k3

R101 k1 k2tog (k1 yo skp yo skp k1 k2tog yo k2tog yo k2) repeat ( ) three more times, (k1 yo skp yo skp k1 k2tog yo k2tog yo k1) k2tog k1 **k1** k1 k2tog (k1 yo skp yo skp k1 k2tog yo k2tog yo k2) repeat ( ) three more times, (k1 yo skp yo skp k1 k2tog yo k2tog yo k1) k2tog k1

R102 k2 (k2 yo k2tog yo k3tog yo k2togb yo k2) (k1 k2 yo k2tog yo k3tog yo k2togb yo k2) repeat ( ) three more times, k2 **k1** k2 (k2 yo k2tog yo k3tog yo k2togb yo k2) (k1 k2 yo k2tog yo k3tog yo k2togb yo k2) repeat ( ) three more times, k2

R103 k1 k2tog (k2 yo skp k1 k2tog yo k3 k1) (k3 yo skp k1 k2tog yo k3 k1) repeat ( ) two more times, (k3 yo skp k1 k2tog yo k2) k2tog k1 **k1** k1 k2tog (k2 yo skp k1 k2tog yo k3 k1) (k3 yo skp k1 k2tog yo k3 k1) repeat ( ) two more times, (k3 yo skp k1 k2tog yo k2) k2tog k1

R104 k1 (k4 yo k3tog yo k4) (k1 k4 yo k3tog yo k4) repeat ( ) two more times, (k1 k4 yo k3tog yo k3) k2 **k1** k1 (k4 yo k3tog yo k4) (k1 k4 yo k3tog yo k4) repeat ( ) two more times, (k1 k4 yo k3tog yo k3) k2

Chart of the Medallion pattern in rows 97-104 on the right hand side of the shawl

---

SEPARATION ROWS

R105 k1 k2tog k55 k2tog k1 **k1** k1 k2tog k55 k2tog k1

R106 k

R107 k1 k2tog k53 k2tog k1 **k1** k1 k2tog k53 k2tog k1

R108 k

BEAD STITCH

R109 k1 k2tog k1 k2 (yo sskp yo k3) repeat ( ) six more times, yo sskp yo k2 k1 k2tog k1 **k1** k1 k2tog k1 k2 (yo sskp yo k3) repeat ( ) six more times, yo sskp yo k2 k1 k2tog k1

R110 k3 k1 (k2tog yo k1 yo k2tog k1) repeat ( ) seven more times, k3 **k1** k3 k1 (k2tog yo k1 yo k2tog k1) repeat ( ) seven more times, k3

R111 k1 k2tog k2tog (yo k3 yo sskp) repeat ( ) six more times, yo k3 yo k2tog k2tog k1 **k1** k1 k2tog k2tog (yo k3 yo sskp) repeat ( ) six more times, yo k3 yo k2tog k2tog k1

R112 k2 k1 (yo k2tog k1 k2tog yo k1) repeat ( ) seven more times, k2 **k1** k2 k1 (yo k2tog k1 k2tog yo k1) repeat ( ) seven more times, k2

R113 k1 k2tog k1 (yo sskp yo k3) repeat ( ) six more times, yo sskp yo k1 k2tog k1 **k1** k1 k2tog k1 (yo sskp yo k3) repeat ( ) six more times, yo sskp yo k1 k2tog k1

R114 k2 (k2tog yo k1 yo k2tog k1) repeat ( ) seven times, k1 **k1** k2 (k2tog yo k1 yo k2tog k1) repeat ( ) seven times, k1

R115 k1 k2tog k3 yo sskp (yo k3 yo sskp) repeat ( ) five more times, yo k3 k2tog k1 **k1** k1 k2tog k3 yo sskp (yo k3 yo sskp) repeat ( ) five more times, yo k3 k2tog k1

R116 k3 k1 k2tog yo k1 (yo k2tog k1 k2tog yo k1) repeat ( ) five more times, yo k2tog k1 k3 **k1** k3 k1 k2tog yo k1 (yo k2tog k1 k2tog yo k1) repeat ( ) five more times, yo k2tog k1 k3

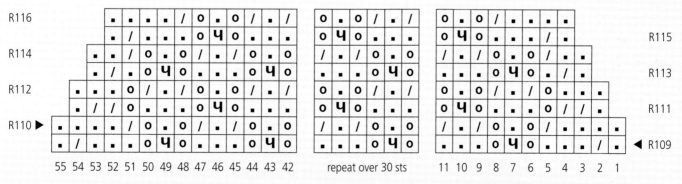

Chart of the Bead Stitch pattern in rows 109-116 on the right hand side of the shawl

SEPARATION ROWS

R117 k1 k2tog k43 k2tog k1 **k1** k1 k2tog k43 k2tog k1

R118 k

R119 k1 k2tog k41 k2tog k1 **k1** k1 k2tog k41 k2tog k1

R120 k

LACE PEBBLES

R121 k1 k2tog k2 (k2tog yo yo k2tog) repeat ( ) eight more times, k1 k2tog k1 **k1** k1 k2tog k2 (k2tog yo yo k2tog) repeat ( ) eight more times, k1 k2tog k1

R122 k3 (k1, k1 p1 into loops, k1) repeat ( ) eight more times, k4 **k1** k3 (k1, k1 p1 into loops, k1) repeat ( ) eight more times, k4

R123 k1 k2tog k3 (k2tog yo yo k2tog) repeat ( ) seven more times k2 k2tog k1 **k1** k1 k2tog k3 (k2tog yo yo k2tog) repeat ( ) seven more times k2 k2tog k1

R124 k4 (k1, k1 p1 into loops, k1) repeat ( ) seven more times, k5 **k1** k4 (k1, k1 p1 into loops, k1) repeat ( ) seven more times, k5

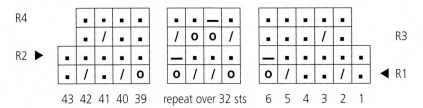

Chart of the Lace Pebbles pattern in rows 121-124 on the right hand side of the shawl

---

SEPARATION ROWS

R125 k1 k2tog k35 k2tog k1 **k1** k1 k2tog k35 k2tog k1

R126 k

R127 k1 k2tog k33 k2tog k1 **k1** k1 k2tog k33 k2tog k1

R128 k

VANDYKE

R129 k1 k2tog k3 (k1 p1 k1 into next st, k3tog) repeat ( ) five more times, k4 k2tog k1 **k1** k1 k2tog k3 (k1 p1 k1 into next st, k3tog) repeat ( ) five more times, k4 k2tog k1

R130 k

R131 k1 k2tog k2 (k3tog, k1 p1 k1 into next st) repeat ( ) five more times, k3 k2tog k1 **k1** k1 k2tog k2 (k3tog, k1 p1 k1 into next st) repeat ( ) five more times, k3 k2tog k1

R132 k

R133 k1 k2tog k1 (k1 p1 k1 into next st, k3tog) repeat ( ) five more times, k2 k2tog k1 **k1** k1 k2tog k1 (k1 p1 k1 into next st, k3tog) repeat ( ) five more times, k2 k2tog k1

R134 k

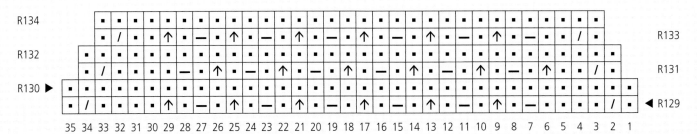

Chart of the Vandyke pattern in rows 129-134 on the right hand side of the shawl

SEPARATION ROWS

R135 k1 k2tog k25 k2tog k1 **k1** k1 k2tog k25 k2tog k1

R136 k

EYELID

R137 k1 k2tog k1 (k1 k2tog yo k1 yo k2tog k1) repeat ( ) two more times, k1 k2tog k1 **k1** k1 k2tog k1 (k1 k2tog yo k1 yo k2tog k1) repeat ( ) two more times, k1 k2tog k1

R138 k3 (k2tog yo k3 yo k2tog) repeat ( ) two more times, k3 **k1** k3 (k2tog yo k3 yo k2tog) repeat ( ) two more times k3

R139 k1 k2tog k21 k2tog k1 **k1** k1 k2tog k21 k2tog k1

R140 k2 (k1 yo k2tog yo k3tog yo k1) repeat ( ) two more times, k2 **k1** k2 (k1 yo k2tog yo k3tog yo k1) repeat ( ) two more times, k2

R141 k1 k2tog k19 k2tog k1 **k1** k1 k2tog k19 k2tog k1

R142 k1 (k2 yo k3tog yo k2) repeat ( ) two more times, k1 **k1** k1 (k2 yo k3tog yo k2) repeat ( ) two more times, k1

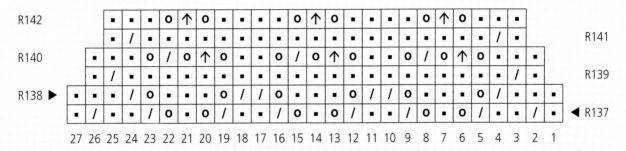

Chart of the Eyelid pattern in rows 137-142 on the right hand side of the shawl

SEPARATION ROWS

R143 k1 k2tog k17 k2tog k1 **k1** k1 k2tog k17 k2tog k1

R144 k

R145 k1 k2tog k15 k2tog k1 **k1** k1 k2tog k15 k2tog k1

R146 k

LACE HOLES

R147 k1 k2tog k1 (k2tog yo k2tog) repeat ( ) two more times, k2tog k1 **k1** k1 k2tog k1 (k2tog yo k2tog) repeat ( ) two more times, k2tog k1

R148 k2 (k1, k1 p1 into loop, k1) repeat ( ) two more times, k3 **k1** k2 (k1, k1 p1 into loop, k1) repeat ( ) two more times, k3

R149 k1 k2tog k11 k2tog k1 **k1** k1 k2tog k11 k2tog k1

R150 k

R151 k1 k2tog k1 (k2tog yo k2tog) repeat ( ) one more time, k2tog k1 **k1** k1 k2tog k1 (k2tog yo k2tog) repeat ( ) one more time, k2tog k1

R152 k2 (k1, k1 p1 into loop, k1) repeat ( ) one more time, k3 **k1** k2 (k1, k1 p1 into loop, k1) repeat ( ) one more time, k3

R153 k1 k2tog k7 k2tog k1 **k1** k1 k2tog k7 k2tog k1

R154 k

R155 k1 k2tog k1 k2tog k2tog yo k2tog k1 **k1** k1 k2tog k1 k2tog yo k2tog k2tog k1

R156 k2 k1, k1 p1 into loop, k1 k3 **k1** k2 k1, k1 p1 into loop, k1 k3

ENDING

R157 k1 k2tog k3 k2tog k1 **k1** k1 k2tog k3 k2tog k1

R158 k

R159 k1 k2tog k1 k2tog k1 k1 **k1** k2tog k1 k2tog k1

R160 k

Bo all sts

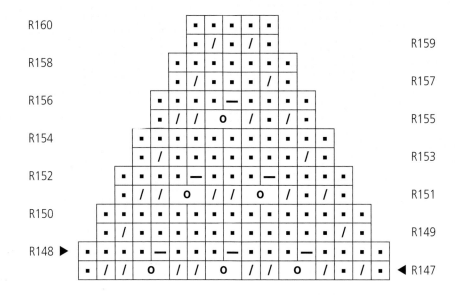

Chart of the Lace holes and ending of the pattern (rows 147-160) on the right hand side of the shawl.
A single yo rather than two yos are used in the lace hole pattern to provide smaller holes. This is illustrated
by having the yo over two sts in the row below. Two sts are knitted into this yo on the next row.

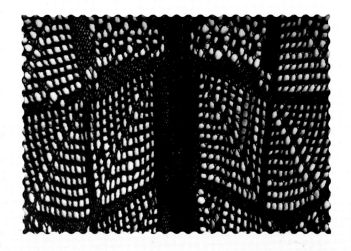
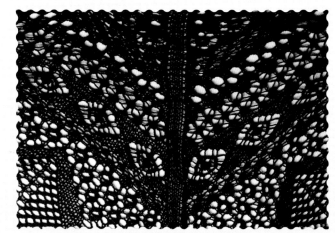

"Celtic Dreams" Circular Shawl

MATERIALS
• 14 balls Patons Grace Yarn, Natural. 50g ball (125 m/ 136 yd)

NEEDLES
• US 6 (4 mm) circular (40", 32" and 24": change when ready to move down to a smaller length), 6 (4 mm) straight needles (pair), US 5 (3.75 mm) circular, US 5 (3.75 mm) double pointed (set of 5), stitch markers, blunt ended needle for weaving in ends

SIZE
• 60" diameter

Instructions

BORDER

The border has 6 pattern sections: boundaries between sections are indicated by a ♦, making it easier to keep track of the different sections. See also the note on Pattern Formats in the Techniques section. In the center, when a new ball is used, yarn should be spliced (see the section elsewhere on practice). The pattern has short rows (R2, R3, R8, R9, R12, R13, R18, R19) to create a curvature of the border. On the border section, any time you need to join to a new ball, do so at the beginning of the straight edge row where the first stitches are knit. This allows for weaving in the ends invisibly.

Co 57 sts on US 6 straight needles
Purl one row

R1 k3 ♦ k1 k2tog yo k1 yo k2tog k2 ♦ k2tog k11 k2tog ♦ k6 yo k2togb k2 yo k2togb k6 ♦ k1 yo k2tog ♦ k2tog (yo k2tog) repeat ( ) 3 times

R2 p10 sts, turn, leaving remaining 44 sts unworked

R3 k2tog (yo k2tog) repeat ( ) 3 times, leave remaining 44 sts unworked

R4 p8 ♦ k1 yo k2tog ♦ p18 ♦ p13 ♦ k1 k2tog yo k3 yo k2tog ♦ k3

R5 k3 ♦ k8 ♦ k2tog k2tog (yo k1) repeat ( ) 4 times, yo k2tog k2tog ♦ k4 k2tog yo k1 yo k2togb k2 yo k2togb k5 ♦ k1 yo k2tog ♦ k1 (yo k2tog) repeat ( ) 2 times, yo k1

R6 p9 ♦ k1 yo k2tog ♦ p18 ♦ p15 ♦ k2 yo k2tog yo k3tog yo k1 ♦ k3

R7 k3 ♦ k8 ♦ k2tog k11 k2tog ♦ k3 k2tog yo k3 yo k2togb k2 yo k2togb k4 ♦ k1 yo k2tog ♦ k2 (yo k2tog) repeat ( ) 2 times, yo k1

R8 p10 ♦ k1 yo k2tog ♦ p18 ♦ p12, turn, leaving remaining 12 sts unworked

R9 k1 k2tog (yo k1) repeat ( ) 4 times, yo k2tog k2tog ♦ k2 k2tog yo k2 k2tog yo k1 yo k2togb k2 yo k2togb k3 ♦ k1 yo k2tog ♦ k3 (yo k2tog) repeat ( ) 2 times, yo k1

R10 p11 ♦ k1 yo k2tog ♦ p18 ♦ p14 p2tog ♦ k3 yo k3tog yo k2 ♦ k3

R11 k3 ♦ k1 k2tog yo k1 yo k2tog k2 ♦ k2tog k11 k2tog ♦ k1 k2tog yo k2 k2tog yo k3 yo k2togb k2 yo k2togb k2 ♦ k1 yo k2tog ♦ k4 (yo k2tog) repeat ( ) 2 times, yo k1

R12 p13, turn, leaving 44 sts unworked

R13 k6 (yo k2tog) repeat ( ) 2 times, yo k1

R14 p13 ♦ k1 yo k2tog ♦ p18 ♦ p13 ♦ k1 k2tog yo k3 yo k2tog ♦ k3

R15 k3 ♦ k8 ♦ k2tog k2tog (yo k1) repeat ( ) 4 times, yo k2tog k2tog ♦ k3 yo k2togb k2 yo k2togb yo k2tog yo k2 k2tog yo k2tog k1 ♦ k1 yo k2tog ♦ k3 k2tog (yo k2tog) repeat ( ) 3 times

(continued on page 118)

(continued from page 116)

R16 p12 ♦ k1 yo k2tog ♦ p18 ♦ p15 ♦ k2 yo k2tog yo k3tog yo k1 ♦ k3

R17 k3 ♦ k8 ♦ k2tog k11 k2tog ♦ k4 yo k2togb k2 yo sskp yo k2 k2tog yo k3 ♦ k1 yo k2tog ♦ k2 k2tog (yo k2tog) repeat ( ) 3 times

R18 p11 ♦ k1 yo k2tog ♦ p18 ♦ p12, turn, leaving remaining 12 sts unworked

R19 k1 k2tog (yo k1) repeat ( ) 4 times, yo k2tog k2tog ♦ k5 yo k2togb k2 yo k2togb k1 k2tog

yo k4 ♦ k1 yo k2tog ♦ k1 k2tog (yo k2tog) repeat ( ) 3 times

R20 p10 ♦ k1 yo k2tog ♦ p18 ♦ p14 p2tog ♦ k3 yo k3tog yo k2 ♦ k3

Repeat R1–R20 52 more times

Knit 1 row

Bo all sts

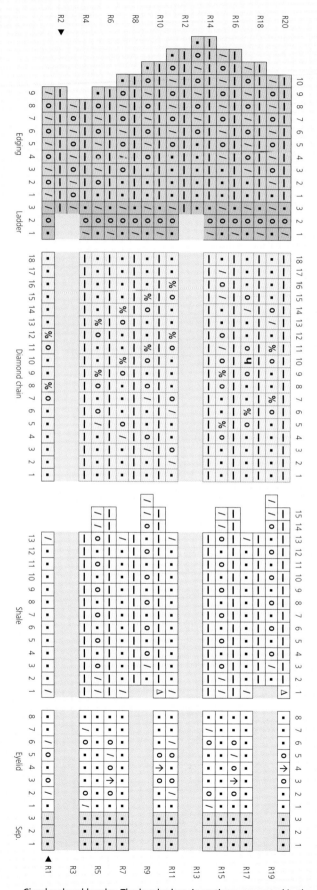

Circular shawl border. The border has six sections, separated in the pattern by ♦ symbols. Sep: Separator stitches to separate the border from the middle of the shawl

MARKING THE CENTER

The 53 repeats have 12 rows on the inner edge, giving 636 rows. From these 636 rows, 480 sts are picked up along the straight edge. This is a key part of the shawl construction. There are eight sections and these sections occur in pairs for picking up, with a Zig-Zag section being followed by a Diamond Chain section. There are therefore four pairs with 120 sts in each, picked up over 159 rows. Sections should be marked with stitch markers. Interlock them to make chains of two or three as required.

There is only one small seam on the shawl. In order for it to be as unobtrusive as possible, the seam will lie at the bottom of the shawl. For the seam to be centered on the bottom Diamond Chain section, this requires that the section be picked up with half the stitches from the beginning of the border and half from the end. The first stitch to be picked up will therefore start on row 41 of the border.

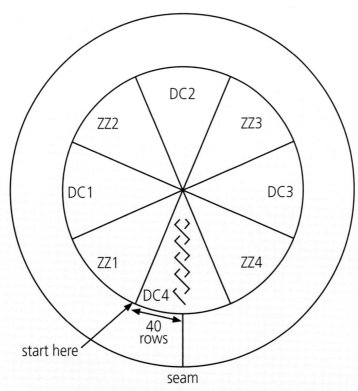

Chart showing the layout of the shawl with eight sections inside the border. Rounds of knitting start with Zig-Zag section 1 (ZZ1) followed by Diamond Chain section 1 (DC1), then Zig-Zag 2 (ZZ2) followed by DC2, ZZ3, DC3, ZZ4 and DC4. The starting point of the round in relation to the end of the border is adjusted to ensure the location of the seam at the midpoint of a Diamond Chain section.

MARKERS ARE PLACED AS FOLLOWS:

1 marker: first stitch of section

2 markers: last stitch of section

3 markers: first stitch of round in the center, and is the first stitch of a Zig-Zag section

OPTIONS FOR PLACING THE MARKERS ARE:

Method 1: place stitch markers on the straight edge as you knit the border

R40 (2 markers): marks the end of the last Diamond Chain section; it will be the end of each round of pattern in the center

R41 (3 markers) - R120 (2 markers): 60 sts for the Zig-Zag section will be picked up between these two markers; the marker at R41 will be the start of each round

R121 (1 marker) - R199 (2 markers): 60 sts for the Diamond Chain section will be picked up between these two markers

R200 (1 marker) - R279 (2 markers): 60 sts for the Zig-Zag section will be picked up between these two markers

R280 (1 marker) - R358 (2 markers): 60 sts for the Diamond Chain section will be picked up between these two markers

R359 (1 marker) - R438 (2 markers): 60 sts for the Zig-zag section will be picked up between these two markers

R439 (1 marker) - R517 (2 markers): 60 sts for the Diamond Chain section will be picked up between these two markers

R518 (1 marker) - R597 (2 markers): 60 sts for the Zig-zag section will be picked up between these two markers

R598 (1 marker) to R636 and the bo row, together with the first 40 rows at the beginning of the border, gives 80 rows from which 60 sts for the last Diamond Chain section will be picked up.

Stitches are picked up using the US 6 circular needle, 3 sts for every 4 rows, with an additional stitch picked up in the middle of each section marked with an underline. A total 480 sts are picked up around the circle.

Mehod 2: place stitch markers once the border is complete. This method is based on counting garter stitch rows which form ridges, with one ridge for every two rows.

Ridge 20 (2 markers): marks the end of the last Diamond Chain section; it will be the end of each round of pattern in the center

Ridge 21 (3 markers) - Ridge 60 (2 markers): 60 sts for the Zig-Zag section will be picked up between these two markers; the marker at ridge 21 will be the start of each round of knitting of the center

Ridge 100 (2 markers): 60 sts for the Diamond Chain section will be picked up between this position and the previous marker

Ridge 140 (2 markers): 60 sts for the Zig-Zag section will be picked up between this position and the previous marker

Ridge 179 (2 markers): 60 sts for the Diamond Chain section will be picked up between this position and the previous marker

Ridge 219 (2 markers): 60 sts for the Zig-Zag section will be picked up between this position and the previous marker

Ridge 258 (2 markers): 60 sts for the Diamond Chain section will be picked up between this position and the previous marker

Ridge 298 (2 markers): 60 sts for the Zig-Zag section will be picked up between this position and the previous marker

From the last marker to R636 and the bo row, together with the first 20 ridges at the beginning of the border, gives 80 rows from which 60 sts for the last Diamond Chain section will be picked up.

Stitches are picked up using the US 6 circular needle, 3 sts for every 4 rows.

ESTABLISHING THE CENTER

Rd in this pattern represents rounds. Counting rounds on circular work can be done with a stitch marker chain. There are already three markers indicating the beginning of a round. Change to a different type of marker from the original three, and every time you start a new round, add a stitch marker to the chain. Once 10 markers have been accumulated, remove them and put them aside and start again with one marker.

Rd1: starting at the 3-marker position, knit one round (480 sts)

Rd2, Eyelet round: (k2tog yo) repeat to end of round, ending with the yo (480 sts)

Rd3: knit (480 sts)

At this point you should have a chain of three round markers added to the initial three.

SPLICING:

It will not be far into the pattern before another ball of yarn will be required. On the next round the Zig-Zag and Diamond Chain sections will begin. It is better to have splicing in the stocking stitch part of the Diamond Chain section, but not on the decrease rows. It should be introduced, if possible, in the first four or five stitches in the section or the last four or five stitches, as it will be integrated into the shaping and avoid the Zig-Zag pattern.

There are eight sections, each knitted from 60 sts of the border. Each round is knitted by alternating the pattern for the Zig-Zag and Diamond Chain sections as indicated for Rounds 1 and 2:

Rd1 [**Zig-Zag** k1 skp (yo k2tog) repeat ( ) 27 more times, k1; **Diamond Chain** k1 skp k18 ♦ k6 yo k2togb k2 yo k2togb k6 ♦ k18 k2tog k1] repeat [ ] three more times.

Rd2 [**Zig-Zag** k59; **Diamond Chain** k20 ♦ k18 ♦ k20] repeat [ ] three more times.

The sections are now in place. Zig-Zag is worked over 8 rounds, Diamond Chain over 16 rounds.

ZIG-ZAG SECTION

ZIG-ZAG SECTION: PART 1 (RD1-RD32)

Rd1 k1 skp (yo k2tog) repeat ( ) 27 more times, k1 (59 sts)

Rd2 k59

Rd3 k2 skp (yo k2tog) repeat ( ) 26 more times, k1 (58 sts)

Rd4 k58

Rd5 k1 skp (yo k2tog) repeat ( ) 26 more times, k1 (57 sts)

Rd6 k57

Rd7 k1 skp (yo k2tog) repeat ( ) 25 more times, k2 (56 sts)

Rd8 k56

Chart showing the first 8 rounds of the Zig-Zag section.
Note: the pattern only decreases at the beginning of each odd-numbered round. It forms a naturally-slanting Zig-Zag.
These eight rounds form the pattern. It forms a distinctive repeating pattern of holes (the blue yos) and ridges (the yellow k2togs).

Repeat Rd1-Rd8 three more times, continuing the decrease pattern at the start of the odd numbered rounds, leaving 44 sts in the section.

EYELID - 1 (RD33-RD42)

Rd1 k44

Rd2 k44

Rd3 k1 (k1 k2tog yo k1 yo k2tog k1) repeat ( ) five more times, k1

Rd4 k1 (k2tog yo k3 yo k2tog) repeat ( ) five more times, k1

Rd5 k1 skp k38 k2tog k1 (42 sts)

Rd6 (k1 yo k2tog yo k3tog yo k1) repeat ( ) five more times

Rd7 k42

Rd8 (k2 yo k3tog yo k2) repeat ( ) five more times
Rd9 k1 skp k36 k2tog k1 (40 sts)
Rd10 k40

Chart (read columns 44 → 1; symbols: · = knit, o = yo, / = k2tog, \ = skp, ↑ = centered double decrease):

```
Cols 44 .................................................. 1          Round
Rd10: · · · · · · · · · · · · · · · · · · · · · · · · · · · · · · · · · · · · · · · · · · · ·   Rd10 / Rd42
Rd9 : · / · · · · · · · · · · · · · · · · · · · · · · · · · · · · · · · · · · · · · · · · \ ·   Rd9  / Rd41
Rd8 :     · · o ↑ o · · · · o ↑ o · · · · o ↑ o · · · · o ↑ o · · · · o ↑ o · · · · o ↑ o · ·   Rd8  / Rd40
Rd7 : · · · · · · · · · · · · · · · · · · · · · · · · · · · · · · · · · · · · · · · · · · · ·   Rd7  / Rd39
Rd6 : · o ↑ o / o · · o ↑ o / o · · o ↑ o / o · · o ↑ o / o · · o ↑ o / o · · o ↑ o / o · · ·   Rd6  / Rd38
Rd5 : · / · · · · · · · · · · · · · · · · · · · · · · · · · · · · · · · · · · · · · · · · \ ·   Rd5  / Rd37
Rd4 : · / o · · o / / o · · o / / o · · o / / o · · o / / o · · o / / o · · o / / o · · o / ·   Rd4  / Rd36
Rd3 : · · / o · o / · · / o · o / · · / o · o / · · / o · o / · · / o · o / · · / o · o / · ·   Rd3  / Rd35
Rd2 : · · · · · · · · · · · · · · · · · · · · · · · · · · · · · · · · · · · · · · · · · · · ·   Rd2  / Rd34
Rd1 : · · · · · · · · · · · · · · · · · · · · · · · · · · · · · · · · · · · · · · · · · · · ·   Rd1  / Rd33

     44 43 42 41 40 39 38 37 36 35 34 33 32 31 30 29 28 27 26 25 24 23 22 21 20 19 18 17 16 15 14 13 12 11 10 9 8 7 6 5 4 3 2 1
```

Chart showing the first Eyelid section within the Zig-Zag section. Both the round number within this part and the overall round number are shown.

ZIG-ZAG SECTION: PART 2 (RD43-RD58)

Rd1 k1 skp (yo k2tog) repeat ( ) 17 more times, k1 (39 sts)

Rd2 k39

Rd3 k2 skp (yo k2tog) repeat ( ) 16 more times, k1 (38 sts)

Rd4 k38

Rd5 k1 skp (yo k2tog) repeat ( ) 16 more times, k1 (37 sts)

Rd6 k37

Rd7 k1 skp (yo k2tog) repeat ( ) 15 more times, k2 (36 sts)

Rd8 k36

Repeat Rd1-Rd8 one more time, leaving 32 sts in the section.

EYELID - 2 (RD59-RD68)

Rd1 k32

Rd2 k32

Rd3 k2 (k1 k2tog yo k1 yo k2tog k1) repeat ( ) three more times, k2

Rd4 k2 (k2tog yo k3 yo k2tog) repeat ( ) three more times, k2

Rd5 k1 skp k26 k2tog k1 (30 sts)

Rd6 k1 (k1 yo k2tog yo k3tog yo k1) repeat ( ) three more times, k1

Rd7 k30

Rd8 k1 (k2 yo k3tog yo k2) repeat ( ) three more times, k1

Rd9 k1 skp k24 k2tog k1 (28 sts)

Rd10 k28

ZIG-ZAG SECTION: PART 3 (RD69-RD80)

Rd1 k1 skp (yo k2tog) repeat ( ) 11 more times, k1 (27 sts)

Rd2 k27

Rd3 k2 skp (yo k2tog) repeat ( ) 10 more times, k1 (26 sts)

Rd4 k26

Rd5 k1 skp (yo k2tog) repeat ( ) 10 more times, k1 (25 sts)

Rd6 k25

Rd7 k1 skp (yo k2tog) repeat ( ) 9 more times, k2 (24 sts)

Rd8 k24 (Rd76)

Rd9 k1 skp (yo k2tog) repeat ( ) 9 more times, k1 (23 sts)

Rd10 k23

Rd11 k2 skp (yo k2tog) repeat ( ) 8 more times, k1 (22 sts)

Rd12 k22 (Rd80)

Zig-Zag section, shawl center (Rd81- Rd 106 on circular US 5 needles)

Note the sskp in Rd21and Rd23

Rd1 k1 skp (yo k2tog) repeat ( ) 8 more times, k1 (21 sts)

Rd2 k21

Rd3 k1 skp (yo k2tog) repeat ( ) 7 more times, k2 (20 sts)

Rd4 k20

Rd5 k1 skp (yo k2tog) repeat ( ) 7 more times, k1 (19 sts)

Rd6 k19

Rd7 k2 skp (yo k2tog) repeat ( ) 6 more times, k1 (18 sts)

Rd8 k18

Rd9 k1 skp (yo k2tog) repeat ( ) 6 more times, k1 (17 sts)

Rd10 k17

Rd11 k1 skp (yo k2tog) repeat ( ) 5 more times, k2 (16 sts)

Rd12 k16

Rd13 k1 skp (yo k2tog) repeat ( ) 5 more times, k1 (15 sts)

Rd14 k15

While knitting Rd15, transfer to a set of five double point US 5 needles, combining a Zig-Zag and a Diamond chain on a single needle and repeat for three more pairs of sections.

Rd15 k2 skp (yo k2tog) repeat ( ) 4 more times, k1 (14 sts)

Rd16 k14

Rd17 k1 skp (yo k2tog) repeat ( ) 4 more times, k1 (13 sts)

Rd18 k13

Rd19 k1 skp (yo k2tog) repeat ( ) 3 more times, k2 (12 sts)

Rd20 k12 (Rd100)

Rd21 k1 sskp k2 (yo k2tog) repeat ( ) one more times, k2 (10 sts)

Rd22 k10

Rd23 k2 sskp k1 yo k2tog k2 (8sts)

Rd24 k1 skp k2tog k1 k2tog (5sts)

Rd25 k1 skp k2 (4 sts)

Rd26 k2tog k2tog

Rd27 k2tog

DIAMOND CHAIN

Rd1 k1 skp k18 ♦ k6 yo k2togb k2 yo k2togb k6 ♦ k18 k2tog k1 (58 sts)

Rd2 k20 ♦ k18 ♦ k20

Rd3 k20 ♦ k4 k2tog yo k1 yo k2togb k2 yo k2togb k5 ♦ k20

Rd4 k20 ♦ k18 ♦ k20

Rd5 k1 skp k17 ♦ k3 k2tog yo k3 yo k2togb k2 yo k2togb k4 ♦ k17 k2tog k1 (56 sts)

Rd6 k19 ♦ k18 ♦ k19

Rd7 k19 ♦ k2 k2tog yo k2 k2tog yo k1 yo k2togb k2 yo k2togb k3 ♦ k19

Rd8 k19 ♦ k18 ♦ k19

Rd9 k1 skp k16 ♦ k1 k2tog yo k2 k2tog yo k3 yo k2togb k2 yo k2togb k2 ♦ k16 k2tog k1 (54 sts)

Rd10 k18 ♦ k18 ♦ k18

Rd11 k18 ♦ k3 yo k2togb k2 yo k2togb yo k2tog yo k2 k2tog yo k2tog k1 ♦ k18

Rd12 k18 ♦ k18 ♦ k18

Rd13 k1 skp k15 ♦ k4 yo k2togb k2 yo sskp yo k2 k2tog yo k3 ♦ k15 k2tog k1 (52 sts)

Rd14 k17 ♦ k18 ♦ k17

Rd15 ♦ k5 yo k2togb k2 yo k2togb k1 k2tog yo k4 ♦

Rd16 k17 ♦ k18 ♦ k17

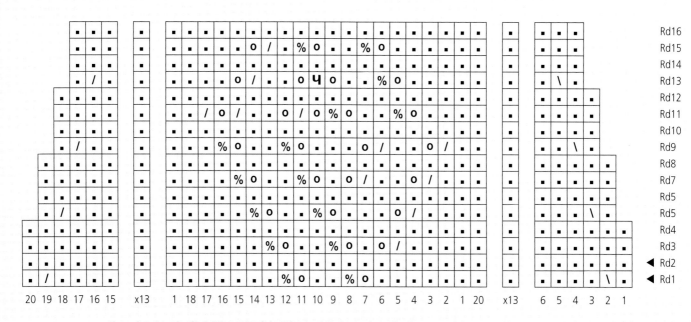

Chart showing the first 16 rounds of the Diamond Chain section. The first row of the section has 58 sts, 20 of the decrease pattern on either side of the 18 st Diamond Chain pattern.

The decrease pattern of 2 sts every 4 rows is now in place on the outer edges of the Diamond Chain section.

Repeat Rd1-Rd16 four more times, continuing the decrease pattern every four rows, leaving 20 sts on the needle. The Diamond Chain pattern ends here and the middle pattern of this section begins.

Diamond Chain section, shawl center (Rd81-Rd107)

Rd27	Rd107
Rd26	Rd106
Rd25	Rd105
Rd24	Rd104
Rd23	Rd103
Rd22	Rd102
Rd21	Rd101
Rd20	Rd100
Rd19	Rd99
Rd18	Rd98
Rd17	Rd97
Rd16	Rd96
Rd15	Rd95
Rd14	Rd94
Rd13	Rd93
Rd12	Rd92
Rd11	Rd91
Rd10	Rd90
Rd9	Rd89
Rd8	Rd88
Rd7	Rd87
Rd6	Rd86
Rd5	Rd85
Rd4	Rd84
Rd3	Rd83
Rd2	Rd82
Rd1	Rd81

18 17 16 15 14 13 12 11 10 9 8 7 6 5 4 3 2 1

Chart showing the last 27 rounds of the Diamond Chain section. Both the round number within this part and the overall round number are shown.

Rd1 k1 skp k14 k2tog k1 (18 sts)

Rd2 k18

Rd3 k3 (k2tog yo yo k2tog) repeat ( ) two more times, k3

Rd4 k3 (k1, k1 p1 into yos, k1) repeat ( ) two more times, k3

Rd5 k1 skp k2 (k2tog yo yo k2tog) repeat ( ) one more time, k2 k2tog k1 (16 sts)

Rd6 k4 (k1, k1 p1 into yos, k1) repeat ( ) one more time, k4

Rd7 k6 k2tog yo yo k2tog k6

Rd8 k6 k1, k1 p1 into yos, k1 k6

Rd9 k1 skp k1 (k2tog yo yo k2tog) repeat ( ) one more time, k1 k2tog k1 (14 sts)

Rd10 k3 (k1, k1 p1 into yos, k1) repeat ( ) one more time, k3

Rd11 k5 k2tog yo yo k2tog k5

Rd12 k5 k1, k1 p1 into yos, k1 k5

Rd13 k1 skp k2 k2tog yo yo k2tog k2 k2tog k1 (12 sts)

Rd14 k4 k1, k1 p1 into yos, k1 k4

Note transfer of the knitting to US 5 double pointed needles, started in the Zig-Zag section, continues here.

Rd15 k4 k2tog yo yo k2tog k4

Rd16 k4 k1, k1 p1 into yos, k1 k4

Rd17 k1 skp k1 k2tog yo yo k2tog k1 k2tog k1 (10 sts)

Rd18 k3 k1, k1 p1 into yos, k1 k3

Rd19 k10

Rd20 k10

Rd21 k1 skp k4 k2tog k1 (8sts)

Rd22 k8

Rd23 k1 skp k2 k2tog k1 (6 sts)

Rd24 k6

Rd25 k1 skp k2tog k1

Rd26 skp k2tog

Rd27 k2tog

SHAWL COMPLETION

Run yarn through the remaining eight sts at the center and weave in. Sew the small seam in the border.

Remove all stitch markers and weave in any other ends.

BLOCKING/DRESSING

Blocking requires some time, but is essential for the final appearance of the shawl. Putting the shawl in water releases the tension in the stitches.

The method I use is:

1. With the temperature of water indicated on the label for washing instructions, briefly put the knitted shawl into a container, ensuring the whole shawl is submerged

2. Drain the water from the container

3. Very gently, squeeze any excess water from the shawl

4. Wrap the shawl in a large clean towel to absorb moisture; when the towel is damp, change to a new towel and repeat until only slightly damp

5. Remove the shawl from the towel and place on a large sheet on the floor

6. In a room where the shawl can air dry as long as needed with the door closed, spread the shawl out to form a good circular shape

7. Beginning with the points on the right hand side of the seam, insert a pin in the first eight peaks; note that **the pins are to support the peak, not to stretch it out**

8. Continuing with the points on the left hand side of the seam, place pins in the first eight peaks

9. Continue working round the shawl alternating sides, pinning eight peaks at a time until all peaks are pinned

Note I do not recommend use of a spray bottle in place of the immersion process described above.

Index

Acknowledgments

Jewelry

Ayala Vitkon
www.ayala-v.co.il
pages 44, 78, 82, 91, 99, 103, 104, 115

Tamara
www.tamara-design.co.il
page 82

Shoes

Shoe Maker
www.shoemaker.co.il
pages 44, 46, 48

UnaUna
www.una-una.com
page 78

Wardrobe

Alona Bar Yona
+972 545 50 70 93
pages 47, 82, 91, 103

Naama Bezalel
www.naamabezalel.com
pages 70, 78, 99, 104, 115

OnebyOne
pages 69